双语名著无障碍阅读丛书
经典集锦

动物农场

Animal Farm

［英国］乔治·奥威尔 著
潘华凌 译

中国出版集团
中译出版社

图书在版编目（CIP）数据

动物农场/（英）奥威尔著；潘华凌译. —北京：中译出版社，
2016.4（2023.2 重印）
（双语名著无障碍阅读丛书）
ISBN 978-7-5001-4601-8

Ⅰ.①动… Ⅱ.①奥… ②潘… Ⅲ.①英语—汉语—对照读物
②童话—英国—近代 Ⅳ.①H319.4：I

中国版本图书馆 CIP 数据核字（2016）第 048067 号

出版发行/中译出版社
地　　址/北京市西城区新街口外大街 28 号普天德胜主楼四层
电　　话/(010) 68359827；68359303（发行部）；68359725（编辑部）
邮　　编/100044
传　　真/(010) 68357870
电子邮箱/book@ ctph.com.cn
网　　址/http：//www.ctph.com.cn

责任编辑/范祥镇　王诗同　杨佳特
封面设计/潘　峰

排　　版/北京竹页文化传媒有限公司
印　　刷/永清县晔盛亚胶印有限公司
经　　销/新华书店

规　　格/710 毫米×1000 毫米　1/16
印　　张/11.75
字　　数/253 千字
版　　次/2016 年 4 月第一版
印　　次/2023 年 2 月第五次

ISBN 978-7-5001-4601-8　　　　　定价：38.00 元

多年以来，中译出版社有限公司（原中国对外翻译出版有限公司）凭借国内一流的翻译和出版实力及资源，精心策划、出版了大批双语读物，在海内外读者中和业界内产生了良好、深远的影响，形成了自己鲜明的出版特色。

二十世纪八九十年代出版的英汉（汉英）对照"一百丛书"，声名远扬，成为一套最权威、最有特色且又实用的双语读物，影响了一代又一代英语学习者和中华传统文化研究者、爱好者；还有"英若诚名剧译丛""中华传统文化精粹丛书""美丽英文书系"，这些优秀的双语读物，有的畅销，有的常销不衰反复再版，有的被选为大学英语阅读教材，受到广大读者的喜爱，获得了良好的社会效益和经济效益。

"双语名著无障碍阅读丛书"是中译专门为中学生和英语学习者精心打造的又一品牌，是一个新的双语读物系列，具有以下特点：

选题创新——该系列图书是国内第一套为中小学生量身打造的双语名著读物，所选篇目均为教育部颁布的语文新课标必读书目，或为中学生以及同等文化水平的社会读者喜闻乐见的世界名著，重新编译为英汉（汉英）对照的双语读本。这些书既给青少年读者提供了成长过程中不可或缺的精神食粮，又让他们领略到原著的精髓和魅力，对他们更好地学习英文大有裨益；同时，丛书中入选的《论语》《茶馆》《家》等汉英对照读物，亦是热爱中国传统文化的中外读者所共知的经典名篇，能使读者充分享受阅读经典的无限乐趣。

无障碍阅读——中学生阅读世界文学名著的原著会遇到很多生词和文化难点。针对这一情况，我们给每一本读物原文中的较难词汇和不易理解之处都加上了注释，在内文的版式设计上也采取英汉（或汉英）对照方式，扫清了学生阅读时的障碍。

优良品质——中译双语读物多年来在读者中享有良好口碑，这得益于作者和出版者对于图书质量的不懈追求。"双语名著无障碍阅读丛书"继承了中译双语读物的优良传统——精选的篇目、优秀的译文、方便实用的注解，秉承着对每一个读者负责的精神，竭力打造精品图书。

愿这套丛书成为广大读者的良师益友，愿读者在英语学习和传统文化学习两方面都取得新的突破。

目
CONTENTS
录

George Orwell

Chapter I

Mr. Jones, of the Manor Farm, had locked the hen-houses for the night, but was too drunk to remember to shut the **potholes**①. With the ring of light from his lantern dancing from side to side, he **lurched**② across the yard, kicked off his boots at the back door, drew himself a last glass of beer from the barrel in the **scullery**③, and made his way up to bed, where Mrs. Jones was already **snoring**④.

As soon as the light in the bedroom went out there was a stirring and a fluttering all through the farm buildings. Word had gone round during the day that old Major, the prize Middle White **boar**⑤, had had a strange dream on the previous night and wished to communicate it to the other animals. It had been agreed that they should all meet in the big barn as soon as Mr. Jones was safely out of the way. Old Major (so he was always called, though the name under which he had been exhibited was Willingdon Beauty) was so highly regarded on the farm that everyone was quite ready to lose an hour's sleep in order to hear what he had to say.

At one end of the big barn, on a sort of raised platform, Major was already **ensconced**⑥ on his bed of straw, under a lantern which hung from a beam. He was twelve years old and had lately grown rather **stout**⑦, but he was still a majestic-looking pig, with a wise and **benevolent**⑧ appearance in spite of the

第一章

① pothole ['pɔthəul] *n.* 坑洞

② lurch [ləːtʃ] *v.* 蹒跚而行

③ scullery ['skʌləri] *n.* 碗碟洗涤室

④ snore [snɔː] *v.* 打鼾

⑤ boar [bɔː] *n.* 公猪

⑥ ensconce [in'skɔns] *v.* 使安躺
⑦ stout [staut] *a.* 粗壮的
⑧ benevolent [bi'nevələnt] *a.* 仁慈的

庄园农场的琼斯先生给鸡舍上了锁，准备过夜。但是，他酒喝多了，醉醺醺的，竟然忘记了把鸡进出的几个小门洞关上。他踉踉跄跄地走过院子，手上提灯投射出的光环也跟着左右摇摆。到了后门口，他便蹬掉了脚上的靴子，从炊具存放室的酒桶里给自己舀出了最后一杯啤酒，喝过之后便准备睡觉去了，而琼斯太太此时已经在床上发出了鼾声。

琼斯先生卧室的灯刚一熄灭，整座农场的各处窝棚内便立刻有了动静，传来一阵振翼拍翅的声响。白天里，消息已经在农场各处传开了，说老少校——那头获过"中白色"奖的公猪——头天夜间做了个怪梦，而且希望把梦的情形告诉给其他动物们。动物们已经说定了，一旦琼斯先生稳稳当当地不碍事了，他们便全部聚集到大谷仓内。老少校（大伙儿一直都这么称呼他来着，不过，他当时参加展览时使用的是"威灵登美男"这个称谓）在农场上享有崇高的威望，所以，每一只动物都很乐意牺牲一个小时睡眠时间来听他讲话。

大谷仓的一端，有一处隆起的台子之类的所在。少校已经安安稳稳地躺在干草铺成的床上，上方悬着一盏固定在横梁上的提灯。他已经十二岁了，最近长得膘肥体壮，但仍不失为是一头仪表堂堂的猪。尽管他的长牙

fact that his **tushes**① had never been cut. Before long the other animals began to arrive and make themselves comfortable after their different fashions. First came the three dogs, Bluebell, Jessie, and Pincher, and then the pigs, who settled down in the straw immediately in front of the platform. The hens **perched**② themselves on the window-sills, the pigeons fluttered up to the **rafters**③, the sheep and cows lay down behind the pigs and began to **chew the cud**④. The two cart-horses, Boxer and Clover, came in together, walking very slowly and setting down their vast hairy hoofs with great care lest there should be some small animal concealed in the straw. Clover was a stout motherly mare approaching middle life, who had never quite got her figure back after her fourth **foal**⑤. Boxer was an enormous beast, nearly eighteen hands high, and as strong as any two ordinary horses put together. A white **stripe**⑥ down his nose gave him a somewhat stupid appearance, and in fact he was not of first-rate intelligence, but he was universally respected for his steadiness of character and tremendous powers of work. After the horses came Muriel, the white goat, and Benjamin, the donkey. Benjamin was the oldest animal on the farm, and the worst tempered. He seldom talked, and when he did, it was usually to make some cynical remark, for instance, he would say that God had given him a tail to keep the flies off, but that he would sooner have had no tail and no flies. Alone among the animals on the farm he never laughed. If asked why, he would say that he saw nothing to laugh at. Nevertheless, without openly admitting it, he was devoted to Boxer; the two of them usually spent their Sundays together in the small **paddock**⑦ beyond the **orchard**⑧, grazing side by side and never speaking.

The two horses had just lain down when a brood of ducklings, which had lost their mother, filed into the barn, **cheeping**⑨ **feebly**⑩ and wandering from

① tush [tʌʃ] *n.* 犬齿

② perch [pɜ:tʃ] *v.* 使暂歇

③ rafter ['rɑ:ftə] *n.* 椽（子）

④ chew the cud 反刍

⑤ foal [fəul] *n.*（尤指不满一岁的马、骡的）驹

⑥ stripe [straip] *n.* 斑纹

⑦ paddock ['pædək] *n.* 小牧场

⑧ orchard ['ɔ:tʃəd] *n.* 果园

⑨ cheep [tʃi:p] *v.* 唧唧地叫

⑩ feebly ['fi:bli] *ad.* 柔弱地

从来没有割剪过，但面相仍然睿智慈祥。不一会儿，其他动物开始陆续到达，按照各自的方式舒舒服服地安顿下来。最先到达的是三条狗：蓝铃、杰西和平彻。随后是几头猪，他们在台子前面的干草上安顿了下来。母鸡们栖身在窗台上，鸽子们展翅飞上了椽子。绵羊和母牛们在猪的后面躺下，并且开始反刍了起来。两匹拉车的马——拳击手和首蓿——一同进入。他们步履缓慢，毛茸茸的宽大蹄子小心翼翼向下踩踏，生怕干草里面藏着某一只小动物。首蓿是一匹膘肥体壮的母马，正接近中年，打从产下第四胎幼崽之后，就再也没有恢复过昔日的体形了。拳击手是一匹高大的马，差不多有十八个一手之宽[1]，力量相当于两匹普通马加在一块儿。一道白色条纹顺着鼻梁而下，让他看上去显得有点傻乎乎。事实上，他的智力并非一流，但是，他性格坚韧不拔，干活儿时体力强盛，因此受到广泛尊敬。马匹之后进入的是白山羊穆里尔和毛驴本杰明。本杰明是农场里年事最高的动物，也是脾气最暴躁的动物。他话很少，但一旦开口说话，定是满口揶揄挖苦的话，比如，他会说，上帝赐予了他一根尾巴，目的是用来驱赶苍蝇的，但是，他宁可不要尾巴，宁可没有苍蝇。动物当中，唯有他是从来不笑的。若是要问为什么，他会回答说，他并没有看见什么可笑的东西。然而，虽说没有公开承认，他却是十分倾心于拳击手。他们二位往往会在果园那边的一片小牧场上度过星期日，肩并肩一块儿吃草，默默无言。

两匹拉车的马刚刚躺了下来，便有一群失去了母亲的小鸭子涌入大谷仓。他们有气无力地唧唧叫着，忽左

---

1 一手之宽（hand）是一种测量马匹高度等的单位，相当于四英寸。文学作品中常常会出现英美制的长度和面积单位，常见的有英里、码、英尺、英寸、平方英里、英亩、平方码、平方英尺等：一英里（mile）等于1.6093千米，一码（yard）等于0.9144米，一英尺（foot）等于0.3048米，一英寸（inch）等于2.54厘米，一平方英里（square mile）等于2.59平方千米，一英亩（acre）等于4047平方米，一平方码（square yard）等于0.8361平方米，一平方英尺（square foot）等于929.03平方厘米。

side to side to find some place where they would not be **trodden**① on. Clover made a sort of wall round them with her great foreleg, and the ducklings nestled down inside it and **promptly**② fell asleep. At the last moment, Mollie, the foolish, pretty white mare who drew Mr. Jones's trap, came **mincing**③ **daintily**④ in, chewing at a lump of sugar. She took a place near the front and began **flirting**⑤ her white **mane**⑥, hoping to draw attention to the red ribbons it was plaited with. Last of all came the cat, who looked round, as usual, for the warmest place, and finally squeezed herself in between Boxer and Clover; there she **purred**⑦ contentedly throughout Major's speech without listening to a word of what he was saying.

All the animals were now present except Moses, the tame **raven**⑧, who slept on a **perch**⑨ behind the back door. When Major saw that they had all made themselves comfortable and were waiting attentively, he cleared his throat and began:

"Comrades, you have heard already about the strange dream that I had last night. But I will come to the dream later. I have something else to say first. I do not think, comrades, that I shall be with you for many months longer, and before I die, I feel it my duty to pass on to you such wisdom as I have acquired. I have had a long life, I have had much time for thought as I lay alone in my stall, and I think I may say that I understand the nature of life on this earth as well as any animal now living. It is about this that I wish to speak to you.

"Now, comrades, what is the nature of this life of ours? Let us face it: our lives are miserable, laborious, and short. We are born, we are given just so much food as will keep the breath in our bodies, and those of us who are capable of it are forced to work to the last atom of our strength; and the very instant that our usefulness has come to an end we are **slaughtered**⑩ with **hideous**⑪ cruelty. No animal in England knows the meaning of happiness or leisure after he is a year old. No animal in England is free. The life of an animal is misery and slavery: that is the plain truth.

① trodden ['trɔdən]（tread 的过去分词）v. 践踏

② promptly ['prɔm(p)tli] ad. 迅速地

③ mincing ['minsiŋ] a. 装模作样的

④ daintily ['deintili] ad. 讲究地

⑤ flirt [fləːt] v. 挥动（尾巴）

⑥ mane [mein] n. 鬃毛

⑦ purr [pəː] v. 猫喘音

⑧ raven ['reivən] n.【鸟类】渡鸦

⑨ perch [pəːtʃ] n. 悬挂东西的横条

⑩ slaughter ['slɔːtə] v. 屠宰

⑪ hideous ['hidiəs] a. 令人惊骇的

忽右地向前走着，想要寻觅一处不被别的动物踩踏到的地方。苜蓿用自己粗大的前腿给小鸭们形成一道像是围墙一样的屏障。而小鸭们则舒适地在屏障里面安顿了下来，很快便睡着了。到了最后时刻，替琼斯先生拉车的莫莉这才忸怩作态地姗姗来迟，这是匹傻乎乎但容貌俏丽的白色母马。她嘴里嚼着一块方糖，在靠前的位置找了一处地方，然后开始抖动着自己的白色鬃毛，卖弄着风情，旨在让大伙儿瞩目她那系在鬃毛上的红色饰带。最后到达的是那只母猫。她和平常一样，左顾右盼，想要寻找一处最温暖的所在，最后挤在了拳击手和苜蓿之间。少校说话期间，她一直心满意足地在那儿发着呼噜声，少校说了什么，她一句也没有听进去。

所有动物现在都到齐了，只有摩西除外，即那只驯化了的渡鸦，他在后门口的栖息架上睡觉来着。少校看到所有动物都舒舒服服地安顿下来，聚精会神地等待着。这时候，他清了清嗓子，开始说话了：

"同志们，你们已经听说过了，我昨晚做了个怪梦。但是，梦的事情我随后再说。我首先要说点别的事情。同志们，我想我和你们待在一块儿的时间不会很长了。在死之前，我觉得有责任把我获得的智慧传给你们。我已经享受了很长的寿命，独自躺在圈栏时，有很多时间进行思考。我认为，自己可以说理解了在这个世界上生命的性质，理解的深度不亚于如今活着的任何动物。我现在想要对你们说的就是关于这个问题。

"对了，同志们，我们的生命性质如何呢？让我们面对它吧：我们活得痛苦不堪，艰辛劳累，寿命短暂。我们生下来，得到的食物只够维持生存，然而，只要我们一息尚存，便会被迫劳作，直到精疲力竭。一旦到了不中用的时刻，我们便会被残忍地宰杀掉。英国的任何动物，只要到了一岁的年龄，便不知道快乐和闲暇是什么意思。英国的任何动物都是不自由的。一只动物的一生是艰难困苦的，饱受奴役的。这是显而易见的事实啊。

"But is this simply part of the order of nature? Is it because this land of ours is so poor that it cannot afford a **decent**① life to those who dwell upon it? No, comrades, a thousand times no! The soil of England is fertile, its climate is good, it is capable of affording food in abundance to an enormously greater number of animals than now inhabit it. This single farm of ours would support a dozen horses, twenty cows, hundreds of sheep, and all of them living in a comfort and a dignity that are now almost beyond our imagining. Why then do we continue in this **miserable**② condition? Because nearly the whole of the produce of our labour is stolen from us by human beings. There, comrades, is the answer to all our problems. It is summed up in a single word—Man. Man is the only real enemy we have. Remove Man from the scene, and the root cause of hunger and overwork is abolished for ever.

"Man is the only creature that consumes without producing. He does not give milk, he does not lay eggs, he is too weak to pull the **plough**③, he cannot run fast enough to catch rabbits. Yet he is lord of all the animals. He sets them to work, he gives back to them the bare minimum that will prevent them from starving, and the rest he keeps for himself. Our labour **tills**④ the soil, our **dung**⑤ fertilises it, and yet there is not one of us that owns more than his bare skin. You cows that I see before me, how many thousands of gallons of milk have you given during this last year? And what has happened to that milk which should have been breeding up **sturdy**⑥ **calves**⑦? Every drop of it has gone down the throats of our enemies. And you hens, how many eggs have you laid in this last year, and how many of those eggs ever **hatched**⑧ into chickens? The rest have all gone to market to bring in money for Jones and his men. And you, Clover,

① decent ['di:sənt] *a.* 体面的

"但是，这难道纯粹是大自然秩序的一部分吗？难道是因为我们的这片土地过于贫瘠，不能让生活在这里的动物们体体面面地过日子吗？不是啊，同志们，绝对不是啊！英国的土地很肥沃，英国的气候很适宜，可以提供丰富的食物，足以养活比现在生活在这里的更加多的动物。仅仅就本农场而言，可以供养十二匹马、二十头牛和几百只羊，全部都可以生活得很舒适，很有尊严，但这种状态现在是无法想象的。而我们为何持续生活在这种悲惨的处境中呢？因为我们劳动的成果几乎全部都被人类窃取了。同志们，我们的全部问题都有答案啦。可以归结为一个字——人。人是我们唯一真正的敌人。把人从现在的世界中驱逐出去，导致我们忍饥挨饿和过度劳累的祸根便永远消除了。

② miserable ['mizərəbl] *a.* 悲惨的；痛苦的

"人类是唯一只会消费不会生产的生灵。他们不能提供奶，不会下蛋；过于孱弱，不能犁地；跑不快，逮不着兔子。然而，他们却是所有动物的主人。他们迫使动物们劳动，而回报给动物的东西却少之又少，只要不饿死就行，剩下的都被他们攫为己有。我们用自己的劳力耕耘着土地，我们用自己的粪便让土地肥沃，但是，我们除了一身皮毛却一无所有。站在我前面的几头奶牛，你们去年产了多少千加仑¹奶呢？那些本该把小牛犊喂得健壮的奶到哪儿去了呢？每一滴奶都进入到了我们的敌人的喉咙管。你们这些母鸡，你们去年下了多少枚蛋呢？那些蛋有多少枚孵成了小鸡呢？其余那些全部都拿到市场上去卖了，给琼斯和他那一帮人换成了钱。

③ plough [plau] *n.* 犁

④ till [til] *v.* 耕，犁
⑤ dung [dʌŋ] *n.* 粪

⑥ sturdy ['stə:di] *a.* 强壮的
⑦ calf [kɑ:f] *n.* 小牛

⑧ hatch [hætʃ] *v.* 孵化

1 此处加仑（gallon）为英美液量单位，一加仑等于四夸脱或八品脱，即英制的 4.546 升，美制的 3.785 升。容量单位有干量（dry measure）和液量（liquid measure）之分，英美的容量单位折合成公制时有所差别，例如：一（干量）夸脱等于英制的 1.136 升，美制的 1.101 升；一（液量）夸脱等于英制的 1.136 升，美制的 0.946 升。一（干量）蒲式耳（bushel）等于英制的 36.368 升，美制的 35.239 升，一（干量）加仑（gallon，仅用于英制）等于 4.546 升。一（液量）加仑等于英制 4.546 升，美制 3.785 升。一（干量）品脱（pint）等于英制 0.568 升，美制 0.55 升，一（液量）品脱等于英制 0.568 升，美制 0.473 升。

where are those four foals you bore, who should have been the support and pleasure of your old age? Each was sold at a year old—you will never see one of them again. In return for your four **confinements**① and all your labour in the fields, what have you ever had except your bare rations and a stall?

"And even the miserable lives we lead are not allowed to reach their natural span. For myself I do not **grumble**②, for I am one of the lucky ones. I am twelve years old and have had over four hundred children. Such is the natural life of a pig. But no animal escapes the cruel knife in the end. You young **porkers**③ who are sitting in front of me, every one of you will scream your lives out at the block within a year. To that horror we all must come—cows, pigs, hens, sheep, everyone. Even the horses and the dogs have no better fate. You, Boxer, the very day that those great muscles of yours lose their power, Jones will sell you to the **knacker**④, who will cut your throat and boil you down for the foxhounds. As for the dogs, when they grow old and toothless, Jones ties a brick round their necks and drowns them in the nearest pond.

"Is it not **crystal clear**⑤, then, comrades, that all the evils of this life of ours spring from the tyranny of human beings? Only get rid of Man, and the produce of our labour would be our own. Almost overnight we could become rich and free. What then must we do? Why, work night and day, body and soul, for the **overthrow**⑥ of the human race! That is my message to you, comrades: Rebellion! I do not know when that Rebellion will come, it might be in a week or in a hundred years, but I know, as surely as I see this straw beneath my feet, that sooner or later justice will be done. Fix your eyes on that, comrades, throughout the short remainder of your lives! And above all, pass on this message of mine to those who come after you, so that future generations shall carry on the struggle until it is **victorious**⑦.

① confinement
[kən'fainmənt] *n.* 分娩

② grumble ['grʌmbl] *v.* 发牢
骚

③ porker ['pɔːkə] *n.* 猪（尤指
食用猪、小猪）

④ knacker ['nækə] *n.* 收买
（或屠宰）老病家畜（废
马等）的人

⑤ crystal clear 极其明白，
十分清楚

⑥ overthrow [ˌəuvə'θrəu] *n.*
推翻，打倒

⑦ victorious [vik'tɔːriəs] *a.* 胜
利的

还有你，苜蓿，你产下的那四匹小马驹到哪儿去了，他
们本来应该成为你老年时的依靠和快乐来着？每一匹都
在一岁时给卖掉了——你再也见不到他们中的任何一匹
啦。你生了四胎，在地里劳作，除了一点点少得可怜的
饲料和一间厩棚，你得到了什么回报呢？

"再说了，我们虽然过着悲惨的生活，但连这样的
生活我们都不允许自然而然地走到生命的尽头。至于我
自己，我没有什么可抱怨的，因为我算是幸运者中的一
位。我已经十二岁了，养育了超过四百个孩子。这算是
一头猪本来享有的寿命了。但是，任何动物最终都逃脱
不掉那把残酷的刀。坐在我前面的这些小猪，一年之内，
你们每一个都会在挨宰之前发出尖叫。我们一定要面对
那恐怖的场景——牛、猪、鸡、羊，每一位。连马和狗
的命运都好不到哪儿去。你，拳击手，等到你强壮的躯
体失去力量的那一天，琼斯便会把你卖给收购老弱马匹
的人，那些人先把你宰杀了，然后再把你煮熟喂猎狐
犬。至于狗，等到他们老了没有牙齿了时，琼斯便会在
他们的脖子上绑砖头，把他们沉到附近的池塘里 面去。

"这么说来，同志们，我们此生悲惨的生活状态源
自人类的暴行，这不是再清楚不过的事情吗？只要摆脱
掉了人类，我们劳动的成果就属于我们自己了。几乎在
一夜之间，我们就会变得富有和自由。那么，我们该怎
么办呢？是啊，要夜以继日、全心全意地干活儿，为的
是推翻人类！这就是我要传递给你们的信息，同志们：
起来反抗！我不知道反抗运动什么时候到来，有可能
一个星期之后，也有可能一百年之后。但我知道，如同我
看见自己脚下的这些干草一样看得真切，正义迟早会得
到伸张。同志们，在你们短暂的余生当中，一定要紧
盯着这个目标啊！而最重要的是，把我的这个信息传递
给你们身后的来者，以便将来一代接一代地斗争下去，
直到最后取得胜利。

"要记住啊，同志们，你们的决心绝不能够动摇。

"And remember, comrades, your resolution must never **falter**①. No argument must lead you **astray**②. Never listen when they tell you that Man and the animals have a common interest, that the prosperity of the one is the prosperity of the others. It is all lies. Man serves the interests of no creature except himself. And among us animals let there be perfect unity, perfect comradeship in the struggle. All men are enemies. All animals are comrades."

At this moment there was a tremendous **uproar**③. While Major was speaking four large rats had crept out of their holes and were sitting on their **hindquarters**④, listening to him. The dogs had suddenly caught sight of them, and it was only by a swift dash for their holes that the rats saved their lives. Major raised his **trotter**⑤ for silence.

"Comrades," he said, "here is a point that must be settled. The wild creatures, such as rats and rabbits—are they our friends or our enemies? Let us put it to the vote. I propose this question to the meeting: Are rats comrades?"

The vote was taken at once, and it was agreed by an overwhelming majority that rats were comrades. There were only four **dissentients**⑥, the three dogs and the cat, who was afterwards discovered to have voted on both sides. Major continued:

"I have little more to say. I merely repeat, remember always your duty of **enmity**⑦ towards Man and all his ways. Whatever goes upon two legs is an enemy. Whatever goes upon four legs, or has wings, is a friend. And remember also that in fighting against Man, we must not come to resemble him. Even when you have conquered him, do not adopt his **vices**⑧. No animal must ever live in a house, or sleep in a bed, or wear clothes, or drink alcohol, or smoke tobacco, or touch money, or engage in trade. All the habits of Man are evil. And, above all, no animal must ever tyrannise over his own kind. Weak or strong, clever or simple, we are all brothers. No animal must ever kill any other animal. All animals are equal.

"And now, comrades, I will tell you about my dream of last night. I cannot

① falter ['fɔːltə] v. 犹豫，迟疑
② astray [ə'strei] ad. 入歧途

③ uproar ['ʌprɔː] n. 骚动

④ hindquarter ['haind,kwɔːtə] n. [用复数]（动物的）后腿和臀部
⑤ trotter ['trɔtə] n. 猪蹄

⑥ dissentient [di'senʃənt] n. 反对者

⑦ enmity ['enməti] n. 敌意，仇恨

⑧ vice [vais] n. 恶习，恶行

一定不能让花言巧语把你们引入歧途。他们若是对你们说，人类和动物是利益共同体，一方富有了，另一方也会富有，决不能听这样的说教。那全都是谎言。人类绝不可能替除自己之外的任何生灵谋取福利。我们动物们在进行斗争的时候必须要完全团结一致，建立起真正的同志情谊。所有人类都是敌人。所有动物都是同志。"

这时，一阵巨大的骚动传来。原来在少校说话的当儿，四只大耗子从洞穴里爬了出来，蹲坐在地上倾听他说话。几条狗看见了他们，多亏耗子动作敏捷，一个箭步冲进了洞穴，这才保全了性命。少校抬起一只蹄子，示意大家保持安静。

"同志们啊，"他说，"这里有一个问题必须要做出决断。诸如耗子和兔子这一类野生动物——他们是我们的朋友呢，还是我们的敌人？我们来对此进行表决吧。我把这个问题在大会上提出来：耗子是同志吗？"

他们立刻进行了表决，多数的动物同意，耗子是同志。只有四票反对，即那三条狗和那只猫。事后发现，他们既投了反对票，也投了赞成票。少校继续说：

"我没有更多的话要说了，只是要重申一下，永远铭记你们承担的责任，要敌视人类及其种种行为。但凡两条腿走路的都是敌人，但凡四条腿走路或者长着翅膀的都是朋友。同时还要牢牢记住，同人类的斗争中，我们决不可以学他们的样子。即便等到你们征服他们了，也不得仿效他们的种种恶行。任何动物都不得居住在房舍里，或者睡在床上，或者穿上衣服，或者饮酒，或者吸烟，或者接触金钱，或者进行贸易。人类的全部习惯都是邪恶的。还有，最重要的，任何动物都不得对同类实施残暴行为。无论屠弱还是强壮，聪颖智慧还是单纯愚笨，我们都是兄弟。任何动物都决不能杀戮其他动物。所有动物都是平等的。

"现在，同志们，我要把我昨晚做的那个怪梦告诉给大家。我无法描述梦的情景，那是关于人类消亡之后

describe that dream to you. It was a dream of the earth as it will be when Man has **vanished**[1]. But it reminded me of something that I had long forgotten. Many years ago, when I was a little pig, my mother and the other **sows**[2] used to sing an old song of which they knew only the **tune**[3] and the first three words. I had known that tune in my **infancy**[4], but it had long since passed out of my mind. Last night, however, it came back to me in my dream. And what is more, the words of the song also came back—words, I am certain, which were sung by the animals of long ago and have been lost to memory for generations. I will sing you that song now, comrades. I am old and my voice is hoarse, but when I have taught you the tune, you can sing it better for yourselves. It is called *Beasts of England*."

Old Major cleared his throat and began to sing. As he had said, his voice was hoarse, but he sang well enough, and it was a stirring tune, something between *Clementine* and *La Cucaracha*. The words ran:

Beasts of England, beasts of Ireland,
Beasts of every land and **clime**[5],
Hearken to my joyful tidings
Of the golden future time.

Soon or late the day is coming,
Tyrant Man shall be o'erthrown,
And the fruitful fields of England
Shall be trod by beasts alone.

Rings shall vanish from our noses,
And the **harness**[6] from our back,
Bit[7] and **spur**[8] shall rust forever,
Cruel **whips**[9] no more shall crack.

① vanish ['vænɪʃ] v. 消失

② sow [sau] n. 老母猪

③ tune [tjuːn] n. 曲调
④ infancy ['infənsi] n. 幼年

地球的景象的。但是，这场梦让我想起了遗忘很久的一些事情。许多年前，我当时还是一头小猪，母亲和另外几头母猪经常哼唱一支古老的歌。她们只会哼唱那支歌曲调和头三句词。我还在襁褓中时便熟悉那曲调了，但后来时间一长便忘记了。然而，昨晚，我在梦中想起了那支歌曲。而且，我竟然连歌词也想起来了——我可以肯定，那些歌词是动物们很久以前唱出的，而且失传了几代。我现在就把这支歌唱给你们听吧，同志们。我上了年纪了，嗓子沙哑了，但是，等到我把曲调教给你们之后，你们自己能够唱得更加悦耳动听。歌名叫作《英格兰的牲畜》。"

老少校清了清嗓子，开始唱了。正如他说的那样，他的嗓子沙哑了，但唱得还是挺好的，旋律慷慨激昂，有介于《克莱门汀》和《拉库库拉恰》之间的韵味。歌词如下：

⑤ clime [klaim] n. 地带，
地区

英格兰的牲畜，爱尔兰的牲畜，
四面八方的牲畜们啊，来吧，
都来倾听我唱一曲，
金色未来的美好光景。

或迟或早，那个日子定会到来，
一定要推翻残暴的人类，
英格兰果实累累的沃土上，
一定只有动物的足迹。

⑥ harness ['hɑːnis] n. 马具，
挽具
⑦ bit [bit] n.（马）嚼子，
马衔
⑧ spur [spəː] n. 踢马刺
⑨ whip [hwip] n. 鞭子

穿过我们鼻子的铁环一定会去掉，
我们背上套着的鞍具也将卸下，
嚼子和马刺将永远生锈，
残酷的皮鞭永不抽响。

富有的情形无法想象，

Riches more than mind can picture,

Wheat and **barley**①; oats and hay;

Clover②, beans, and **mangel-wurzels**③

Shall be ours upon that day.

Bright will shine the fields of England,

Purer shall its waters be,

Sweeter yet shall blow its breezes

On the day that sets us free.

For that day we all must labour,

Though we die before it break;

Cows and horses, geese and turkeys,

All must **toil**④ for freedom's sake.

Beasts of England, beasts of Ireland,

Beasts of every land and clime,

Hearken well and spread my tidings

Of the golden future time.

The singing of this song threw the animals into the wildest excitement. Almost before Major had reached the end, they had begun singing it for themselves. Even the stupidest of them had already picked up the tune and a few of the words, and as for the clever ones, such as the pigs and dogs, they had the entire song by heart within a few minutes. And then, after a few **preliminary**⑤ tries, the whole farm burst out into *Beasts of England* **in tremendous unison**⑥. The cows **lowed**⑦ it, the dogs **whined**⑧ it, the sheep **bleated**⑨ it, the horses **whinnied**⑩ it, the ducks **quacked**⑪ it. They were so delighted with the song that they sang it right through five times in succession, and might have continued singing it all night if they had not been interrupted.

① barley ['bɑːli] *n.* 大麦
② clover ['kləuvə] *n.* 【植】苜蓿
③ mangel-wurzel ['mæŋɡəl,wəːzl] *n.* 饲料甜菜，糖萝卜

小麦和大麦，燕麦和干草，
苜蓿，大豆，还有甜菜，
到那一天统统归我们所有。

英格兰的田野上阳光明媚，
流淌着的水更加纯净，
吹拂过的风更加和煦，
那一天，我们享有自由。

为了那一天，我们必须劳作，
哪怕是未见黎明身先死。
无论奶牛马匹，鹅群火鸡，
为了自由，拼命干吧。

④ toil [tɔil] *v.* 辛勤劳动

英格兰的牲畜，爱尔兰的牲畜，
四面八方的牲畜啊，来吧，
都来倾听我唱一曲，
金色未来的美好光景。

唱出的歌声让动物们无比兴奋，激动不已。少校几乎都还没有来得及唱到结尾处时，他们自己便已经开始唱起来了。连其中最愚笨的动物都已经学会了曲调旋律和几句歌词。至于那些聪颖智慧的，如猪和狗，他们几分钟时间便熟记了全部歌词。这时候，经过几次试唱之后，整座农场突然爆发出了《英格兰的牲畜》嘹亮的合唱声。奶牛哞哞低吟，狗汪汪长吠，绵羊咩咩和声，马匹嘶鸣献唱，鸭子嘎嘎唱响。他们兴高采烈唱着歌，连着唱了五遍。如果不是被打断了，他们准会彻夜唱下去。

⑤ preliminary [pri'liminəri] *a.* 预备（性）的
⑥ in unison 一致地
⑦ low [ləu] *v.* （牛）哞哞叫
⑧ whine [hwain] *v.* 发呜咽声
⑨ bleat [bliːt] *v.* 咩咩叫
⑩ whinny ['hwini] *v.* （马）鸣
⑪ quack [kwæk] *v.* （鸭子）发出嘎嘎声

Unfortunately, the uproar awoke Mr. Jones, who sprang out of bed, making sure that there was a fox in the yard. He seized the gun which always stood in a corner of his bedroom, and let fly a charge of number 6 shot into the darkness. The **pellets**[①] buried themselves in the wall of the barn and the meeting broke up hurriedly. Everyone fled to his own sleeping-place. The birds jumped on to their perches, the animals settled down in the straw, and the whole farm was asleep in a moment.

① pellet ['pelit] *n.* 子弹

　　不幸的是，喧闹的歌声惊醒了琼斯先生。他一骨碌从床上爬起来，想弄清楚院落里是不是进了狐狸。他抓起一直摆放在卧室角落里的那支猎枪，朝着黑暗中射出了一梭子六型号的子弹。子弹射进了谷仓的墙壁，动物们的聚会很快散掉了。每只动物都迅速逃回到自己的睡觉处。鸟儿飞上了自己栖息架，其他动物在干草堆里躺下。整个农场瞬间进入了梦乡。

Chapter II

Three nights later old Major died peacefully in his sleep. His body was buried at the foot of the orchard.

This was early in March. During the next three months there was much secret activity. Major's speech had given to the more intelligent animals on the farm a completely new outlook on life. They did not know when the Rebellion predicted by Major would take place, they had no reason for thinking that it would be within their own lifetime, but they saw clearly that it was their duty to prepare for it. The work of teaching and organising the others fell naturally upon the pigs, who were generally recognised as being the cleverest of the animals. **Pre-eminent**① among the pigs were two young boars named Snowball and Napoleon, whom Mr. Jones was breeding up for sale. Napoleon was a large, rather fierce-looking Berkshire boar, the only Berkshire on the farm, not much of a talker, but with a reputation for getting his own way. Snowball was a more **vivacious**② pig than Napoleon, quicker in speech and more inventive, but was not considered to have the same depth of character. All the other male pigs on the farm were porkers. The best known among them was a small fat pig named Squealer, with very round cheeks, **twinkling**③ eyes, **nimble**④ movements, and a **shrill**⑤ voice. He was a brilliant talker, and when he was arguing some difficult point he had a way of **skipping**⑥ from side to side and **whisking**⑦ his tail which

第二章

三个夜晚之后，少校在睡眠中安详地离世了。他的遗体掩埋在果园的下面。

那是三月初的事情。随后的三个月当中，秘密活动不断。少校的一席话给了农场上那些更加聪慧的动物们极大的鼓舞，让他们对生命有了全新的看法。他们不知道，少校预言的反抗运动何时会发生。他们没有理由认为，自己的有生之年内，运动会发生。但是，他们心里很清楚，为那场运动做准备，这是他们的义务。教育和组织其他动物的工作自然而然地落到了猪的肩上，因为动物们普遍认为，他们是所有动物中最聪颖智慧的。猪当中称得上卓越的是两头名叫雪球和拿破仑的小公猪。他们是琼斯先生饲养了要去卖的。拿破仑体形硕大，相貌凶狠，属于伯克郡猪种，是农场上唯一的伯克郡猪，话不多，但出了名的我行我素。相对于拿破仑，雪球性情更加活泼，口齿更加伶俐，思维更加敏捷，但大家觉得，他性格不那么深沉。农场上所有别的公猪都是肉猪。他们当中最出名的是一头名叫尖嗓子的小肥猪，滚瓜溜圆的脸颊，闪闪发亮的眼睛，动作敏捷，声音尖细。他说话伶牙俐齿，每当针对疑难问题辩论说理时，身子左蹦右跳，尾巴摆来摆去，让说的话多少显得很有说服力。大家说起尖

① pre-eminent [pri'eminənt] *a.* 优秀的，杰出的

② vivacious [vi'veiʃəs] *a.* 活泼的

③ twinkling ['twiŋkliŋ] *a.* 闪烁的；闪亮的
④ nimble ['nimbl] *a.* 敏捷的
⑤ shrill [ʃril] *a.* 尖声的
⑥ skip [skip] *v.* 跳来跳去
⑦ whisk [hwisk] *v.* 挥动

was somehow very persuasive. The others said of Squealer that he could turn black into white.

These three had **elaborated**① old Major's teachings into a complete system of thought, to which they gave the name of Animalism. Several nights a week, after Mr. Jones was asleep, they held secret meetings in the barn and **expounded**② the principles of Animalism to the others. At the beginning they met with much stupidity and **apathy**③. Some of the animals talked of the duty of loyalty to Mr. Jones, whom they referred to as "Master," or made **elementary**④ remarks such as "Mr. Jones feeds us. If he were gone, we should starve to death." Others asked such questions as "Why should we care what happens after we are dead?" or "If this Rebellion is to happen anyway, what difference does it make whether we work for it or not?", and the pigs had great difficulty in making them see that this was contrary to the spirit of Animalism. The stupidest questions of all were asked by Mollie, the white mare. The very first question she asked Snowball was: "Will there still be sugar after the Rebellion?"

"No," said Snowball firmly. "We have no means of making sugar on this farm. Besides, you do not need sugar. You will have all the oats and hay you want."

"And shall I still be allowed to wear ribbons in my mane?" asked Mollie.

"Comrade," said Snowball, "those ribbons that you are so devoted to are the **badge**⑤ of slavery. Can you not understand that liberty is worth more than ribbons?"

Mollie agreed, but she did not sound very convinced.

The pigs had an even harder struggle to counteract the lies put about by Moses, the tame raven. Moses, who was Mr. Jones's especial pet, was a spy and a tale-bearer, but he was also a clever talker. He claimed to know of the existence of a mysterious country called Sugarcandy Mountain, to which all animals went when they died. It was situated somewhere up in the sky, a little distance beyond the clouds, Moses said. In Sugarcandy Mountain it was Sunday

嗓子时，都说他能够把黑的说成白的。

上面提到的三头猪殚精竭虑，让老少校的教诲形成了一套完整的思想体系。他们给这个思想体系取名为"动物思想"。一个星期有几个晚上的时间，等到琼斯先生睡觉了之后，他们便会在谷仓里举行秘密会议，给其他动物详细阐述动物思想的原则。刚开始时，听他们讲解的动物冥顽不化，无动于衷。有些动物还谈到了要履行忠实于琼斯先生的义务，他们把他称为"主人"。他们或者说些很没有水平的话，诸如"琼斯先生给我们饭吃，他若是不在了，我们就得饿死"。另外一些动物提出种种问题，诸如"我们为何要在意自己死了之后会发生什么事情呢"或者"假如反抗运动迟早会爆发，我们是否为之劳作那又有什么关系呢"？因此，几头猪费尽了口舌，旨在让他们明白，这样的说法是与动物思想的精髓相违背的。莫莉提出了最愚不可及的问题："反抗运动爆发之后，还有糖吃吗？"

"没有，"雪球说，语气很坚定，"我们没有办法在本农场制糖。再说了，你也不需要糖。你可以享用你想要的燕麦和干草。"

"还允许我在鬃毛上系饰带吗？"莫莉问了一声。"同志啊，"雪球说，"你一门心思迷恋的那些饰带可是奴役的标志啊。你难道就不明白自由的价值远高于饰带吗？"

莫莉表示认同，但说话的声音听起来并不那么心悦诚服。

那只驯化了的渡鸦摩西满嘴谎言。几头猪要戳穿那些谎言，需要进行更加艰难的斗争。摩西是琼斯先生格外宝贝的宠物。他善于刺探信息，搬弄是非，而且还是个巧言令色的说客。他声称自己知道世界上有个名叫糖果山的神秘地方，所有动物死后都会去那儿。那地方在天空中的某处，距离云层不远，摩西就是这么说来着。糖果山上，一星期七天都是星期日，苜蓿四季常青，一

① elaborate [i'læbəreit] v. 详尽阐述

② expound [ik'spaund] v. （详细）说明，阐明

③ apathy ['æpəθi] n. 无动于衷

④ elementary [ˌeli'mentəri] a. 初级的

⑤ badge ['bædʒ] n. 标识，标记

seven days a week, clover was in season all the year round, and **lump**[①] sugar and **linseed**[②] cake grew on the hedges. The animals hated Moses because he told tales and did no work, but some of them believed in Sugarcandy Mountain, and the pigs had to argue very hard to persuade them that there was no such place.

Their most faithful **disciples**[③] were the two cart-horses, Boxer and Clover. These two had great difficulty in thinking anything out for themselves, but having once accepted the pigs as their teachers, they absorbed everything that they were told, and passed it on to the other animals by simple arguments. They were unfailing in their attendance at the secret meetings in the barn, and led the singing of *Beasts of England*, with which the meetings always ended.

Now, as it turned out, the Rebellion was achieved much earlier and more easily than anyone had expected. In past years Mr. Jones, although a hard master, had been a capable farmer, but **of late**[④] he had **fallen on evil days**[⑤]. He had become much disheartened after losing money in a lawsuit, and had taken to drinking more than was good for him. For whole days at a time he would **lounge**[⑥] in his Windsor chair in the kitchen, reading the newspapers, drinking, and occasionally feeding Moses on **crusts**[⑦] of bread soaked in beer. His men were idle and dishonest, the fields were full of weeds, the buildings wanted roofing, the hedges were neglected, and the animals were **underfed**[⑧].

June came and the hay was almost ready for cutting. On Midsummer's Eve, which was a Saturday, Mr. Jones went into Willingdon and got so drunk at the Red Lion that he did not come back till midday on Sunday. The men had milked the cows in the early morning and then had gone out rabbiting, without bothering to feed the animals. When Mr. Jones got back he immediately went to sleep on the drawing-room sofa with the *News of the World* over his face, so that when evening came, the animals were still unfed. At last they could stand it no longer. One of the cows broke in the door of the store-shed with

① lump [lʌmp] *a.* 成块状的
② linseed ['linsi:d] *n.* 亚麻籽

③ disciple [di'saipl] *n.* 信徒

④ of late 最近；近来
⑤ fall on evil days 倒霉

⑥ lounge [laundʒ] *v.* 虚度
（光阴）
⑦ crust [krʌst] *n.* 面包皮

⑧ underfeed [ˌʌndəˈfiːd]
v. 没喂饱（过去分词
underfed）

道道树篱上长出糖块和亚麻籽饼干[1]。动物们都很仇视摩西，因为他好搬弄是非，不干活儿。但是，他们中有一些相信有"糖果山"这么一处地方。几头猪只好大费口舌，据理力争，说服他们，并没有这么一处地方。

他们最忠实的信徒是那两匹拉车的马，拳击手和苜蓿。这两位怎么努力也思考不出属于自己的东西来，但是，认准了几头猪是自己的老师，他们说什么东西都会一股脑儿接受，而且会以简单要点的形式传授给其他动物。谷仓里举行的秘密会议，他们一如既往，从不缺席。每次会议结束时，他们总是会领唱《英格兰的牲畜》。

然而，事态的发展出乎每一只动物的预料，反抗运动爆发得比大家预想的要更加早，成功的取得也更加容易。过去的岁月中，琼斯先生虽说是位苛刻的主人，却也是位很有能力的农场主。但是，最近，他可是倒了大霉了，惹上了一场官司，赔了钱，弄得够心灰意冷的，于是喝酒往往超量。有时候，一连数天，他懒洋洋地靠坐在厨房里的那把温莎椅上，看看报，喝喝酒，还时不时地把面包屑浸在啤酒里喂给摩西吃。他手下的那帮人无所事事，欺上瞒下，田地里杂草丛生，牲禽的窝棚顶部失修漏雨，树篱无人修剪，动物们吃不饱肚子。

六月到了，草料等着收割。施洗约翰节[2]的前一天是个星期六，琼斯先生去了威灵登，在"红狮"酒吧喝得酩酊大醉，所以一直到星期天的中午才回来。他的手下一大早就挤了牛奶，然后，没有费心思去给动物喂饲料，便跑去猎野兔了。琼斯先生回家后，立刻就在起居室的沙发上睡着了，脸上盖着一份《世界新闻报》。因此，到了黄昏时刻，动物们还是饿着肚子。最后，他们无法忍受下去了。母牛中有一头用角顶开了饲料棚的门，所有动物都开始从一个个饲料仓里自己吃了起来。就在这个当儿，琼斯先生醒过来了。片刻之后，他和他的四名

1　亚麻籽饼干（linseed cake）是一种家畜饲料。
2　施洗约翰节（Midsummer's Day）在每年 6 月 24 日。

her horn and all the animals began to help themselves from the **bins**①. It was just then that Mr. Jones woke up. The next moment he and his four men were in the store-shed with whips in their hands, **lashing out**② in all directions. This was more than the hungry animals could bear. With one accord, though nothing of the kind had been planned beforehand, they flung themselves upon their **tormentors**③. Jones and his men suddenly found themselves being **butted**④ and kicked from all sides. The situation was quite out of their control. They had never seen animals behave like this before, and this sudden uprising of creatures whom they were used to **thrashing**⑤ and **maltreating**⑥ just as they chose, frightened them almost **out of their wits**⑦. After only a moment or two they gave up trying to defend themselves and **took to their heels**⑧. A minute later all five of them were in full flight down the cart-track that led to the main road, with the animals pursuing them in triumph.

Mrs. Jones looked out of the bedroom window, saw what was happening, hurriedly flung a few possessions into a carpet bag, and slipped out of the farm by another way. Moses sprang off his perch and flapped after her, **croaking**⑨ loudly. Meanwhile the animals had chased Jones and his men out on to the road and slammed the five-barred gate behind them. And so, almost before they knew what was happening, the Rebellion had been successfully carried through: Jones was expelled, and the Manor Farm was theirs.

For the first few minutes the animals could hardly believe in their good fortune. Their first act was to **gallop**⑩ in a body right round the boundaries of the farm, as though to make quite sure that no human being was hiding anywhere upon it; then they raced back to the farm buildings to wipe out the last traces of Jones's hated reign. The harness-room at the end of the stables was broken open; the bits, the nose-rings, the dog-chains, the cruel knives with which Mr. Jones had been used to **castrate**⑪ the pigs and lambs, were all flung down the well. The reins, the halters, the **blinkers**⑫, the **degrading**⑬ nosebags, were thrown on to the rubbish fire which was burning in the yard. So were the whips. All the animals **capered**⑭ with joy when they saw the whips going up in flames.

① bin [bin] *n.*（贮藏食物的）箱子

② lash out 猛击

③ tormentor [tɔ:'mentə] *n.* 折磨者
④ butt [bʌt] *v.* 猛撞

⑤ thrash [θræʃ] *v.*（用棍、鞭等）痛打
⑥ maltreat [mæl'tri:t] *v.* 虐待
⑦ out of one's wits 不知所措
⑧ take to one's heels 逃之夭夭

⑨ croak [krəuk] *v.* 发嘎嘎声

⑩ gallop ['gæləp] *v.* 飞跑，疾驰

⑪ castrate [kæ'streit] *v.* 阉割
⑫ blinker ['bliŋkə] *n.*（马的）眼罩
⑬ degrading [di'greidiŋ] *a.* 可耻的
⑭ caper ['keipə] *v.* 欢跃，雀跃

员工手里拿着鞭子到了饲料棚，鞭子劈头盖脸从四面八方乱抽了过来。忍饥挨饿的动物们无法忍受这样的鞭抽。虽说动物们事先并无任何计划，但他们一致行动，扑向向他们施暴的人。琼斯先生和他的手下突然发现自己遭受着来自四面八方的角顶脚踢。局面完全失控了。他们先前从未见识过动物有如此表现。过去他们对于动物想抽打就抽打，想虐待就虐待。而现在动物们奋起反抗了，这一招可把他们给吓得魂飞魄散了。仅仅过了一会儿，他们便放弃了抵抗，撒腿跑了。又过了一会儿，动物们大获全胜地在后面跟踪追击，他们五个人则顺着通向大路的马车道狼狈逃窜。

琼斯太太在卧室的窗户口朝着外面张望，看见了正在发生的一幕，便匆忙地把一些财产塞进一个毯制口袋里，顺着另外一条路溜出了农场。摩西一跃身子离开了栖息架，拍打着翅膀一路跟随在她后面，嘴里呱呱地大声叫着。与此同时，动物们追击着琼斯和他的手下到了大路上，砰然关上了有五道闩的大门。因此，动物们几乎还没有来得及弄明白发生了什么情况，反抗运动已经取得了成功。琼斯被驱逐出了农场，庄园农场属于他们了。

开始几分钟里，动物们简直不相信自己的好运。他们的第一个行动就是绕着农场的地界快速跑一圈，好像是为了搞清楚，确实没有人类藏匿在农场的某处。随后，他们跑回农场的窝棚区，清除掉琼斯可恨的统治留下的一切遗迹。坐落在厩棚一端存放挽具处的房门被撞开了。嚼子、鼻环、狗链，琼斯先生常常用来宰杀猪羊的那些残忍刀具，统统被扔到井里面去了。缰绳、笼头、眼罩，有损尊严的挂在动物颈部的饲料袋，全部当作垃圾扔进了在院子里焚烧的火堆里。还有那些鞭子也扔进去了。当动物们看见鞭子化为灰烬时，他们高兴得欢呼雀跃。雪球把那些平常赶集的日子里系在马鬃和马尾上面的饰带也扔进了火堆里。

Snowball also threw on to the fire the ribbons with which the horses' manes and tails had usually been decorated on market days.

"Ribbons," he said, "should be considered as clothes, which are the mark of a human being. All animals should go naked."

When Boxer heard this he fetched the small straw hat which he wore in summer to keep the flies out of his ears, and flung it on to the fire with the rest.

In a very little while the animals had destroyed everything that reminded them of Mr. Jones. Napoleon then led them back to the store-shed and served out a double ration of corn to everybody, with two biscuits for each dog. Then they sang *Beasts of England* from end to end seven times running, and after that they settled down for the night and slept as they had never slept before.

But they woke at dawn as usual, and suddenly remembering the glorious thing that had happened, they all raced out into the **pasture**[①] together. A little way down the pasture there was a **knoll**[②] that **commanded**[③] a view of most of the farm. The animals rushed to the top of it and gazed round them in the clear morning light. Yes, it was theirs—everything that they could see was theirs! In the **ecstasy**[④] of that thought they **gambolled**[⑤] round and round, they hurled themselves into the air in great leaps of excitement. They rolled in the **dew**[⑥], they cropped mouthfuls of the sweet summer grass, they kicked up **clods**[⑦] of the black earth and **snuffed**[⑧] its rich scent. Then they made a tour of inspection of the whole farm and surveyed with speechless admiration the ploughland, the hayfield, the orchard, the pool, the **spinney**[⑨]. It was as though they had never seen these things before, and even now they could hardly believe that it was all their own.

Then they filed back to the farm buildings and halted in silence outside the door of the farmhouse. That was theirs too, but they were frightened to go inside. After a moment, however, Snowball and Napoleon butted the door open with their shoulders and the animals entered in single file, walking with the utmost care for fear of disturbing anything. They tiptoed from room to room, afraid to speak above a whisper and gazing with a kind of **awe**[⑩] at the unbelievable

"饰带，"他说，"应该视同衣服，乃人类的标志。所有动物都是不穿衣服的。"

拳击手听到这么一说后，便去取来了那顶小草帽，那是他夏日里戴着防止苍蝇侵扰自己的耳朵用的，然后把帽子和其他东西一道扔进了火堆里。

一会儿的工夫，动物们销毁了让他们想起琼斯先生的一切器物。拿破仑此时领着他们返回了饲料棚，给每个动物发放了双份饲料，每条狗都拿到了两块饼干。然后，他们唱起了《英格兰的牲畜》，从头至尾唱了七遍。那之后，他们安顿下来过夜了，从来没有这么踏实地睡过。

但是，他们和平常一样在黎明醒来，突然想起了已经发生的光荣事件。他们一块儿跑到外面的牧场。牧场那边的不远处，有一个小山丘，站立在那儿几乎可以看到整座农场的全景。动物们跑到小山丘的顶部，就着清亮的晨间光线，环顾四周。是啊，这一切都属于他们了——他们能够看到的一切都是属于他们的！他们想到这一点便欣喜若狂，一圈又一圈地蹦跳嬉戏着，兴奋得向空中蹿起。他们在露水上打滚，嘴里塞满甘甜鲜润的夏草，把脚下的黑土块踢得四处乱飞，尽情地吸入黑土散发出的芳香。然后，他们把整座农场巡视了一番，默默无语地惊慕着眼前的一切：耕地、草料田、果园、池塘、树丛。他们好像过去从未见过这些东西似的，即便现在，他们也还难以相信，这一切都是属于他们的了。

然后，他们列队返回农场的窝棚区，并且驻足在农场主的住宅外面，默默无语。那儿也是属于他们的了，但是，他们胆战心惊，不敢入内。不过，片刻之后，雪球和拿破仑用肩膀顶开了房门，动物们这才排成一队进入了，格外谨慎，生怕惊动了什么东西。他们踮着脚从一个房间到达另外一个，不敢大声说话，只能轻声细语，充满了敬畏，目不转睛，看着眼前的奢华场面：一张张

① pasture ['pɑ:stʃə] *n.* 牧草地
② knoll [nəul] *n.* 圆丘；土墩
③ command [kə'mɑ:nd] *v.* 俯视

④ ecstasy ['ekstəsi] *n.* 狂喜
⑤ gambol ['gæmbəl] *v.* 跳蹦，雀跃
⑥ dew [dju:] *n.* 露水
⑦ clod [klɔd] *n.* 土块
⑧ snuff [snʌf] *v.* 嗅
⑨ spinney ['spini] *n.* 矮林

⑩ awe [ɔ:] *n.* 敬畏

luxury, at the beds with their feather **mattresses**①, the looking-glasses, the horsehair sofa, the Brussels carpet, the **lithograph**② of Queen Victoria over the drawing-room **mantelpiece**③. They were just coming down the stairs when Mollie was discovered to be missing. Going back, the others found that she had remained behind in the best bedroom. She had taken a piece of blue ribbon from Mrs. Jones's dressing-table, and was holding it against her shoulder and admiring herself in the glass in a very foolish manner. The others **reproached**④ her sharply, and they went outside. Some hams hanging in the kitchen were taken out for burial, and the barrel of beer in the scullery was **stove**⑤ in with a kick from Boxer's hoof, otherwise nothing in the house was touched. A **unanimous**⑥ resolution was passed on the spot that the farmhouse should be preserved as a museum. All were agreed that no animal must ever live there.

The animals had their breakfast, and then Snowball and Napoleon called them together again.

"Comrades," said Snowball, "it is half past six and we have a long day before us. Today we begin the hay harvest. But there is another matter that must be attended to first."

The pigs now revealed that during the past three months they had taught themselves to read and write from an old spelling book which had belonged to Mr. Jones's children and which had been thrown on the rubbish heap. Napoleon sent for pots of black and white paint and led the way down to the five-barred gate that gave on to the main road. Then Snowball (for it was Snowball who was best at writing) took a brush between the two **knuckles**⑦ of his trotter, painted out MANOR FARM from the top bar of the gate and in its place painted ANIMAL FARM. This was to be the name of the farm from now onwards. After this they went back to the farm buildings, where Snowball and Napoleon sent for

① mattress ['mætris] *n.* 床垫；褥子

② lithograph ['liθəugrɑːf] *n.* 平版画

③ mantelpiece ['mæntlpiːs] *n.* 壁炉架

④ reproach [ri'prəutʃ] *v.* 斥责

⑤ stove [stəuv] (stave 的过去式和过去分词) *v.* 穿孔

⑥ unanimous [juːˈnæniməs] *a.* 全体一致的

⑦ knuckle ['nʌkl] *n.* (小牛、猪等的) 肘

铺着羽绒垫的床铺，一面面镜子，马鬃沙发，布鲁塞尔地毯，起居室壁炉架上方挂着的维多利亚女王[1]的石印画像。他们心满意足地从楼上下来，结果发现莫莉不见了。其他动物返回到了楼上发现，她留在那间豪华的卧室内，从琼斯太太的梳妆台上取了一根蓝色饰带，正把饰带贴着自己的肩膀在镜子面前比画着，一副傻乎乎的样子，欣赏着镜子里面自己的尊容。另外一些动物严厉地斥责了她之后就到室外了。他们把挂在厨房里的一些火腿拿去埋掉了。炊具存放室的那只啤酒桶被拳击手的蹄子给踢破了，除此之外，室内的一切都完好无损。他们当即一致通过了一项决议，农场主的住宅应该保留下来辟为博物馆。大家都一致赞同，任何动物都不得入住其中。

动物们用过了早餐。雪球和拿破仑随后再次把他们召集了起来。

"同志们，"雪球说，"现在是六点半，我们还有漫长的一整天呢。我们今天开始收割草料。但是，现在还有另外一件事情，我们必须得首先进行处理。"

几头猪此时透露：过去三个月期间，他们对照着一本陈旧的拼音课本自学了读写技能。那课本原本是琼斯先生的孩子们的，后来被扔到了垃圾堆里。拿破仑派动物去取了几罐黑白涂料，领着大家走向通往大路的那扇五道闩大门。这时候，雪球（因为雪球的字写得最好）用蹄子的两个趾头夹住一把刷子，用涂料把大门顶端横条上的"庄园农场"几个字盖掉，在原处写上"动物农场"。从今往后，这就是这座农场的名字了。这件事情完成之后，他们返回到了农场的窝棚区，雪球和拿破仑

---

1 维多利亚女王（Alexandrina Victoria, 1819 ~ 1901, 1837 ~ 1901 年在位）是英国历史上在位时间最长的一位君主，1837 年 6 月 20 日，年仅十八岁时即位。年轻的女王即位之后展示出了非凡的治国理政的才能，英国的经济迅速发展，文化空前繁荣，海外扩张加速，成为一个强大的帝国。英国有些历史学家称"维多利亚时代"为英国历史上的"黄金时代"。

a ladder which they caused to be set against the end wall of the big barn. They explained that by their studies of the past three months the pigs had succeeded in reducing the principles of Animalism to Seven Commandments. These Seven Commandments would now be **inscribed**① on the wall; they would form an unalterable law by which all the animals on Animal Farm must live for ever after. With some difficulty (for it is not easy for a pig to balance himself on a ladder) Snowball climbed up and set to work, with Squealer a few **rungs**② below him holding the paint-pot. The Commandments were written on the **tarred**③ wall in great white letters that could be read thirty yards away. They ran thus:

THE SEVEN COMMANDMENTS

1. Whatever goes upon two legs is an enemy.
2. Whatever goes upon four legs, or has wings, is a friend.
3. No animal shall wear clothes.
4. No animal shall sleep in a bed.
5. No animal shall drink alcohol.
6. No animal shall kill any other animal.
7. All animals are equal.

It was very neatly written, and except that "friend" was written "freind" and one of the "s" was the wrong way round, the spelling was correct all the way through. Snowball read it aloud for the benefit of the others. All the animals nodded in complete agreement, and the cleverer ones at once began to learn the Commandments by heart.

"Now, comrades," cried Snowball, throwing down the paint-brush, "to the hayfield! Let us make it a point of honour to get in the harvest more quickly than Jones and his men could do."

But at this moment the three cows, who had seemed uneasy for some time past, set up a loud lowing. They had not been milked for twenty-four hours, and their **udders**④ were almost bursting. After a little thought, the pigs sent for

在那儿派动物搬来了一张梯子，他们把梯子靠在谷仓一端的外墙上。几头猪解释说，过去三个月，他们通过学习研究，成功地把动物思想的原则简约成了"七戒"。他们现在要把"七戒"书写在墙壁上，从而构成一部不能更改的法律。所有动物都必须一辈子遵从。雪球费了好一番工夫（因为猪要在梯子上保持身体平衡实属不易）爬上梯子，开始工作。尖嗓子举着涂料罐站立在他身后低几步处。"七戒"用巨大的白色字母写在涂过柏油的墙壁上，三十码以外清晰可辨。内容如下：

① inscribe [inˈskraib] v. 题写

② rung [rʌŋ] n.（梯子的）梯级
③ tar [tɑ:] v. 涂柏油

七 戒

1. 但凡两条腿走路就是敌人。
2. 但凡四条腿走路或者长有翅膀的就是朋友。
3. 任何动物都不穿衣服。
4. 任何动物都不睡在床上。
5. 任何动物都不饮酒。
6. 任何动物都不杀戮别的动物。
7. 所有动物一律平等。

字写得很工整。除了把"朋友"写成了"朋有"，还有一处的笔画写反了，通篇文字都拼写正确。雪球把内容大声念给其他动物听。所有动物都频频点头，表示完全赞同。更加聪颖睿智的动物立刻开始背诵"七戒"。

"好啦，同志们，"雪球大声喊着，一边扔下涂料刷子，"前往草料地！让我们比琼斯和他的雇员更快地收割草料，让这件事情成为一个荣耀吧。"

但是，此时此刻，那三头奶牛哞哞地大声叫了起来，她们有好一会儿都显得焦躁不安。因为她们已经有二十四个小时没有挤奶了，乳房胀得快要爆裂。几头猪思忖片刻后，打发其他动物提来了牛奶桶，很成功地给

④ udder [ˈʌdə] n.（牛、羊等的）乳房

buckets and milked the cows fairly successfully, their trotters being well adapted to this task. Soon there were five buckets of **frothing**[①] **creamy**[②] milk at which many of the animals looked with considerable interest.

"What is going to happen to all that milk?" said someone.

"Jones used sometimes to mix some of it in our **mash**[③]," said one of the hens.

"Never mind the milk, comrades!" cried Napoleon, placing himself in front of the buckets. "That will be attended to. The harvest is more important. Comrade Snowball will lead the way. I shall follow in a few minutes. Forward, comrades! The hay is waiting."

So the animals trooped down to the hayfield to begin the harvest, and when they came back in the evening it was noticed that the milk had disappeared.

① frothing ['frɔθiŋ] *a.* 充满泡沫的
② creamy ['kriːmi] *a.* 奶油色的

③ mash [mæʃ] *n.* 糊状饲料

奶牛挤了奶，他们的蹄子很好地适应了这项工作。不一会儿，他们挤了五桶冒着泡儿的浓牛奶。许多动物饶有兴趣地看着几桶牛奶。

"这些牛奶怎么办啊？"有动物问了一声。

"琼斯有时候会掺一些到我们的饲料里面。"有只母鸡说。

"别管牛奶的事情，同志们！"拿破仑大声说，一边站立到牛奶桶的前面，"这件事情自然会处理妥当的。眼下收割草料更加重要。雪球同志先领头去。我一会儿就去。前进吧，同志们！草料在等待着呢。"

就这样，动物们成群结队地前往草料地，开始了收割行动。他们在黄昏返回时，有人注意到，牛奶不见了。

Chapter III

How they toiled and sweated to get the hay in! But their efforts were rewarded, for the harvest was an even bigger success than they had hoped.

Sometimes the work was hard; the implements had been designed for human beings and not for animals, and it was a great drawback that no animal was able to use any tool that involved standing on his hind legs. But the pigs were so clever that they could think of a way round every difficulty. As for the horses, they knew every inch of the field, and in fact understood the business of **mowing**① and **raking**② far better than Jones and his men had ever done. The pigs did not actually work, but directed and **supervised**③ the others. With their superior knowledge it was natural that they should assume the leadership. Boxer and Clover would harness themselves to the cutter or the horse-rake (no bits or reins were needed in these days, of course) and **tramp**④ steadily round and round the field with a pig walking behind and calling out "**Gee up**⑤, comrade!" or "Whoa back, comrade!" as the case might be. And every animal down to the humblest worked at turning the hay and gathering it. Even the ducks and hens toiled **to and fro**⑥ all day in the sun, carrying tiny **wisps**⑦ of hay in their **beaks**⑧. In the end they finished the harvest in two days' less time than it had usually taken Jones and his men. Moreover, it was the biggest harvest that the farm had ever seen. There was no **wastage**⑨ whatever, the hens and ducks with their sharp

第三章

为了把草料收割进来，他们不辞艰辛，挥洒汗水！但是，他们的努力获得了回报，因为收割行动取得了巨大成功，大大超出了他们的预期。

有时候，要干的活儿很艰难，因为那些农具是替人类而不是替动物设计的。这里出现了一个巨大的障碍，即有些农具要求两条腿站立才能使用，而动物是无法使用的。但是，几头猪很聪明，面对每一个困难，他们总能够想出办法绕过去。至于那些马匹，他们对田地的每一寸都很熟悉。事实上，对于割草和耙地这样的农活，他们比琼斯和他的雇员都干得更加漂亮。猪实际上不干活儿，但负责指挥和监督其他动物劳动。他们凭着自己更加丰富的知识，自然而然承担起了领导的责任。拳击手和苜蓿会给自己套上割草机或马拉耙（当然，现如今，再也无须使用嚼子缰绳了），步伐稳健，一圈又一圈地在地里绕着，有头猪在后面走着，而且会根据情况的不同，大声喊着："加把劲，同志！"或者"喔，退后，同志！"每一只动物都参加了翻草和收割的活动。连鸭子和母鸡都整天在太阳下来回奔忙，辛勤劳作，用嘴衔着少之又少的干草。最后，他们完成了收割任务，比琼斯和他的雇员少用了两天时间。此外，这座农场从未出现过如此喜人的丰收景象。没有一丝一毫的浪费，母鸡和鸭子凭

① mow [məu] *v.* 收割
② rake [reik] *v.* （用耙子）耙
③ supervise ['sju:pəvaiz] *v.* 监督

④ tramp [træmp] *v.* 重力踩
⑤ gee up 让马快跑

⑥ to and fro 来回地
⑦ wisp [wisp] *n.* 小把
⑧ beak [bi:k] *n.* 喙

⑨ wastage ['weistidʒ] *n.* 损失；耗损

eyes had gathered up the very last **stalk**①. And not an animal on the farm had stolen so much as a mouthful.

All through that summer the work of the farm went like clockwork. The animals were happy as they had never conceived it possible to be. Every mouthful of food was an acute positive pleasure, now that it was truly their own food, produced by themselves and for themselves, not **doled out**② to them by a **grudging**③ master. With the worthless **parasitical**④ human beings gone, there was more for everyone to eat. There was more leisure too, inexperienced though the animals were. They met with many difficulties, for instance, later in the year, when they harvested the corn, they had to **tread it out**⑤ in the ancient style and blow away the **chaff**⑥ with their breath, since the farm possessed no **threshing machine**⑦, but the pigs with their cleverness and Boxer with his tremendous muscles always **pulled them through**⑧. Boxer was the admiration of everybody. He had been a hard worker even in Jones's time, but now he seemed more like three horses than one; there were days when the entire work of the farm seemed to rest on his mighty shoulders. From morning to night he was pushing and pulling, always at the spot where the work was hardest. He had made an arrangement with one of the **cockerels**⑨ to call him in the mornings half an hour earlier than anyone else, and would put in some volunteer labour at whatever seemed to be most needed, before the regular day's work began. His answer to every problem, every setback, was "I will work harder!" which he had adopted as his personal motto.

But everyone worked according to his capacity. The hens and ducks, for instance, saved five **bushels**⑩ of corn at the harvest by gathering up the **stray**⑪ grains. Nobody stole, nobody grumbled over his rations, the quarrelling and biting and jealousy which had been normal features of life in the old days had almost disappeared. Nobody **shirked**⑫ or almost nobody. Mollie, it was true, was not good at getting up in the mornings, and had a way of leaving work early on the ground that there was a stone in her hoof. And the behaviour of the cat was somewhat peculiar. It was soon noticed that when there was work to be

① stalk [stɔːk] *n.*（植物的）梗

② dole out（少量地）发放
③ grudging ['ɡrʌdʒiŋ] *a.* 不情愿的，吝啬的
④ parasitical [pærə'sitikl] *a.* 寄生的

⑤ tread out 用脚蹂碾（谷粒等）
⑥ chaff [tʃɑːf] *n.* 谷壳

⑦ threshing machine 脱粒机

⑧ pull through 渡过难关

⑨ cockerel ['kɔkərəl] *n.* 小公鸡

⑩ bushel ['buʃəl] *n.* 蒲式耳（谷物的容量单位）
⑪ stray [strei] *a.* 散落的

⑫ shirk [ʃəːk] *v.* 开小差

着自己敏锐的目光，落下的最后一棵草梗都会收起来。农场上没有一只动物偷吃一口饲料。

整个夏天，农场上的活儿井然有序，像时钟一样精准。动物们幸福愉快，如此情形他们过去无法想象。每吃一口食物他们都会敏锐地感受到真真切切的快乐，因为那实实在在是他们自己的食物，由他们自己生产，为了他们自己生产，而不是由哪个抠门吝啬的主人施舍给他们的。百无一用同时却过着寄生虫生活的人类被驱逐了，每只动物都有更多食物吃。同时也有了更多的闲暇时间，尽管动物们没有经验。他们遇到了许多困难，比如，到了下半年，动物要收获谷物了，由于农场上没有谷物脱粒机，他们只能采用古老的办法，用蹄子踩踏，然后再用嘴吹去谷壳。但是，那些猪凭着自己聪明睿智的脑袋，拳击手凭着自己强壮无比的肌肉，总能克服种种困难。拳击手是人人钦佩的对象。即便在琼斯统治的时代，拳击手也是个卖力干活儿的好手，但是，现如今，他似乎变成了三匹马，而非一匹。有那么一些日子，整座农场上的活儿似乎都落在了他强壮的肩膀上。他从早到晚又是推又是拉的，总是出现在活儿最繁重的地方。他已经同一只小公鸡约定好了，早晨比别的动物提前半小时叫醒他，规定的劳动开始之前，到最需要的地方先干一些义务活儿。面对每一个问题，每一次挫折，他的回答都是："我要更加卖力干活儿！"——他把这句话当作自己的座右铭了。

但是，每一只动物都会干自己力所能及的活儿。比如说母鸡和鸭子吧，他们在收获季节里，收拾散落的谷物，减少了五蒲式耳谷物的损失。没有任何动物偷窃，没有任何动物对自己的饲料配额表达过抱怨。吵架拌嘴，相互撕咬，相互嫉妒，这些昔日生活中的常态，如今全都销声匿迹了。没有任何动物偷懒懈怠——或者说几乎没有。确实，莫莉早晨起床时显得不那么爽快，而且也会以蹄子里面夹了石头为由，提前收工。而那只猫

done the cat could never be found. She would vanish for hours **on end**①, and then reappear at meal-times, or in the evening after work was over, as though nothing had happened. But she always made such excellent excuses, and purred so affectionately, that it was impossible not to believe in her good intentions. Old Benjamin, the donkey, seemed quite unchanged since the Rebellion. He did his work in the same slow **obstinate**② way as he had done it in Jones's time, never shirking and never volunteering for extra work either. About the Rebellion and its results he would express no opinion. When asked whether he was not happier now that Jones was gone, he would say only "Donkeys live a long time. None of you has ever seen a dead donkey," and the others had to be content with this **cryptic**③ answer.

On Sundays there was no work. Breakfast was an hour later than usual, and after breakfast there was a ceremony which was observed every week without fail. First came the **hoisting**④ of the flag, Snowball had found in the harness-room an old green tablecloth of Mrs. Jones's and had painted on it a hoof and a horn in white. This was run up the flagstaff in the farmhouse garden every Sunday morning. The flag was green, Snowball explained, to represent the green fields of England, while the hoof and horn signified the future Republic of the Animals which would arise when the human race had been finally overthrown. After the hoisting of the flag all the animals trooped into the big barn for a general assembly which was known as the Meeting. Here the work of the coming week was planned out and resolutions were put forward and debated. It was always the pigs who put forward the resolutions. The other animals understood how to vote, but could never think of any resolutions of their own. Snowball and Napoleon were by far the most active in the debates. But it was noticed that these two were never in agreement: whatever suggestion either of them made, the other could be counted on to oppose it. Even when it was resolved a thing no one could object to in itself—to set aside the small paddock behind the orchard as a home of rest for animals who were past work, there was a stormy debate over the correct retiring age for each class of animal. The

① on end 连续地

② obstinate ['ɔbstinit] a. 顽强
的

③ cryptic ['kriptik] a. 含义模
糊的

④ hoist [hɔist] v. 升起

的表现显得有那么一点儿奇特。大家很快便就注意到
了，一有活儿要干时，猫便不见了踪影。她往往会一连
几个小时失踪，然后，到了用餐时间，或者傍晚活儿干
完了时，她便又重新冒出来了，好像什么事情都没有发
生过似的。但是，她总是可以找到绝妙的理由，而且呼
噜呼噜，声情并茂，让大家不相信她的良好心思都不
行。打从反抗运动爆发以来，那匹毛驴老本杰明似乎没
有发生什么变化。他如同琼斯统治的时期一样，干活儿
还是那样缓慢而又顽强，从不偷懒，也从不自告奋勇干
额外的活儿。关于反抗运动及其结果，他从不发表任何
看法。当被问到现在琼斯被赶走了，他是否感到高兴时，
他只是会说"驴子寿命很长，你们中任何一位都看不见
驴子的尸体"，面对这个神乎其神的回答，其他动物只
能如此而已。

　　星期天，大家无须干活儿。早餐比平常推后一个小
时。早餐过后，有个仪式，每个星期都要举行，从不间
断。首先是升旗。雪球在挽具房内找到了琼斯太太的一
块旧桌布，并用白色涂料在上面画了一只兽蹄和一个兽
角。每个星期天的早晨，这面旗子就会在农场主住宅花
园里的旗杆上升起来。旗帜是绿色的，雪球解释说，代
表英格兰绿色的田野，而那只兽蹄和那个兽角象征着未
来的动物共和国，那是在人类最终被推翻之后，必将要
诞生的。升旗仪式举行完毕后，动物们成群结队地进入
大谷仓，去参加一个叫作"会议"的大聚会。未来一个
星期的工作在此安排部署，大家提出各种动议，进行讨
论。动议一直都是由几头猪提出来的。其他动物懂得该
如何表决，但从来不考虑提出自己的议案。讨论过程中，
雪球和拿破仑极为活跃。但是，大家注意到，他们二位
从来都不会有一致的看法。他们不管谁提出建议，对方
一定会加以反对。有件事情已经决定了，即把果园后面
那一小片牧场预留给丧失劳动能力的动物建一处养老之
家，此事没有任何动物提出反对意见。即便在这样的情

Meeting always ended with the singing of *Beasts of England*, and the afternoon was given up to **recreation**①.

The pigs had set aside the harness-room as a headquarters for themselves. Here, in the evenings, they studied **blacksmithing**②, carpentering, and other necessary arts from books which they had brought out of the farmhouse. Snowball also busied himself with organising the other animals into what he called Animal Committees. He was **indefatigable**③ at this. He formed the Egg Production Committee for the hens, the Clean Tails League for the cows, the Wild Comrades' Re-education Committee (the object of this was to tame the rats and rabbits), the Whiter Wool Movement for the sheep, and various others, besides instituting classes in reading and writing. On the whole, these projects were a failure. The attempt to tame the wild creatures, for instance, broke down almost immediately. They continued to behave very much as before, and when treated with generosity, simply took advantage of it. The cat joined the Re-education Committee and was very active in it for some days. She was seen one day sitting on a roof and talking to some **sparrows**④ who were just out of her reach. She was telling them that all animals were now comrades and that any sparrow who chose could come and perch on her **paw**⑤; but the sparrows kept their distance.

The reading and writing classes, however, were a great success. By the autumn almost every animal on the farm was literate in some degree.

As for the pigs, they could already read and write perfectly. The dogs learned to read fairly well, but were not interested in reading anything except the Seven Commandments. Muriel, the goat, could read somewhat better than the dogs, and sometimes used to read to the others in the evenings from scraps of newspaper which she found on the rubbish **heap**⑥. Benjamin could read as well as any pig, but never exercised his faculty. So far as he knew, he said, there was nothing worth reading. Clover learnt the whole alphabet, but could not put words together. Boxer could not get beyond the letter D. He would trace out A, B, C, D, in the dust with his great hoof, and then would stand staring at the letters

① recreation [ˌrekriˈeiʃən] *n.* 娱乐

② blacksmithing [ˈblæk.smiθiŋ] *n.* 打铁

③ indefatigable [ˌindiˈfætigəbl] *a.* 不屈不挠的

④ sparrow [ˈspærəu] *n.* 麻雀

⑤ paw [pɔː] *n.* 爪子

⑥ heap [hiːp] *n.* 堆

况下，在确定每一种动物的退休年龄问题上，照样会爆发出暴风雨般的争论。"会议"总是在《英格兰的牲畜》的歌声中结束，下午是娱乐时间。

几头猪把挽具房辟为他们自己的指挥总部。他们把一些书籍从农场主住宅里搬来了，晚上在此从书本上学习铁匠工艺、木匠工艺，还有其他的必要工艺。雪球也在忙着把其他动物组织起来，成立他所谓的"动物委员会"。他干这件事情时可谓不屈不挠。他为母鸡组建了"产蛋委员会"，为奶牛组建了"清洁尾巴社团"，还组建了野生动物的"再教育委员会"（该组织旨在驯化耗子和兔子），还为绵羊发起了"羊毛增白运动"。除了设立各种读写班之外，还有各种各样名头的东西。总体上来说，这些计划项目都失败了。比如，驯化野生动物的计划立刻中断了。他们一如既往，和过去的行为一模一样。而一旦得到了宽容大度的对待，便会尽情地利用这一点。那只猫加入了"再教育委员会"，而且在其中活跃了一些日子。一天，有动物看见，她坐在一个窝棚顶上，对着一些麻雀说话，麻雀处在她够不着的地方。她告诉他们说，所有动物现在都是同志了，麻雀随便哪一只如若愿意都可栖息到她的爪子上。但是，麻雀们还是保持着距离。

不过，读写班还是取得了巨大成功。到了秋季时，农场上的每一只动物都在一定程度上能够识文断字了。

至于那几头猪，他们完全能够读写自如了。狗的阅读能力也相当不错，但是，除了"七戒"之外，他没有兴趣阅读任何材料。比起几条狗，山羊穆里尔的阅读能力要强一些，有时候，夜间会把从垃圾堆里捡来的报纸上的片断读给其他动物听。本杰明的阅读能力不比任何猪差，但就是从来都没有展示过自己的能力。他说，据他所知，没有任何东西值得阅读。苜蓿学会了二十六个英文字母，但就是不会拼字。拳击手认到字母 D 就认不下去了。他能够用自己的大蹄子在泥土上画出 A、B、 with his ears back, sometimes shaking his **forelock**[①], trying with all his might to remember what came next and never succeeding. On several occasions, indeed, he did learn E, F, G, H, but by the time he knew them, it was always discovered that he had forgotten A, B, C, and D. Finally he decided to be content with the first four letters, and used to write them out once or twice every day to refresh his memory. Mollie refused to learn any but the six letters which spelt her own name. She would form these very neatly out of pieces of **twig**[②], and would then decorate them with a flower or two and walk round them admiring them.

None of the other animals on the farm could get further than the letter A. It was also found that the stupider animals, such as the sheep, hens, and ducks, were unable to learn the Seven Commandments by heart. After much thought Snowball declared that the Seven Commandments could in effect be reduced to a single **maxim**[③], namely: "Four legs good, two legs bad." This, he said, contained the essential principle of Animalism. Whoever had thoroughly grasped it would be safe from human influences. The birds at first objected, since it seemed to them that they also had two legs, but Snowball proved to them that this was not so.

"A bird's wing, comrades," he said, "is an organ of **propulsion**[④] and not of **manipulation**[⑤]. It should therefore be regarded as a leg. The distinguishing mark of man is the hand, the instrument with which he does all his **mischief**[⑥]."

The birds did not understand Snowball's long words, but they accepted his explanation, and all the humbler animals set to work to learn the new maxim by heart. FOUR LEGS GOOD, TWO LEGS BAD, was inscribed on the end wall of the barn, above the Seven Commandments and in bigger letters. When they had once got it by heart, the sheep developed a great liking for this maxim, and often as they lay in the field they would all start bleating "Four legs good, two legs bad! Four legs good, two legs bad!" and keep it up for hours on end, never growing tired of it.

Napoleon took no interest in Snowball's committees. He said that the

① forelock ['fɔːlɔk] *n.* 额毛

② twig [twig] *n.* 细枝，嫩枝

③ maxim ['mæksim] *n.* 格言

④ propulsion [prəu'pʌlʃən] *n.* 推进力
⑤ manipulation [mə,nipju'leiʃən] *n.* 操纵
⑥ mischief ['mistʃif] *n.* 危害；祸害

C、D，然后伫立在那儿目不转睛地盯住字母看，两只耳朵朝后竖着，时而抖一抖额毛，设法回想着接下来的字母，但就是想不起来。确实，有好几次，他学会了认 E、F、G、H，等到他熟悉了这几个字母后，却又总是发现，先前认识的 A、B、C、D 又给忘记了。最后，他决定，自己还是满足于头四个字母吧，通常每天书写一两遍，以便记忆。莫莉除了学习拼写自己名字的六个字母[1]之外，拒绝学习任何字母。她用一些树枝的枝条便可以整整齐齐地把六个字母摆出来，然后还会用一两朵花装饰一下，围着它们转圈，得意地欣赏着。

至于农场上的其他动物，没有学了超过字母 A 的。大家还发现，那些更加愚笨的动物们，诸如绵羊、母鸡，还有鸭子，"七戒"的内容都记不住。左思右想之后，雪球宣布，"七戒"实际上可以概括成一句单独的格言，即"四条腿好，两条腿坏"。他说，这句格言涵盖了动物思想的核心原则。无论哪一位，一旦彻底吃透了其精神实质，那就可以稳稳当当地不受人类的影响。禽类一开始时表示反对，因为他们觉得，他们自己也是两条腿的，但雪球向他们证明了，情况并不是这么回事。

"同志们，"他说，"禽类的翅膀是一个起推进作用的器官，而不是起操纵作用的。因此，可以看作是腿。人类起区别作用的标志是手，那可是他们用于使坏的利器啊。"

禽类们听不懂雪球冗长的词汇，但他们接受他的解释，所有更加低等的动物全都着手背诵这条新的格言。"四条腿好，两条腿坏"写在大谷仓的边墙上面，位于"七戒"之上，字体更大。等到他们背下来了之后，绵羊便喜欢上了这条格言。他们躺在田地里时，常常会咩咩地叫起来："四条腿好，两条腿坏！"然后便连续几个小时这样念叨着，从不感到厌烦。

拿破仑对于雪球的各种委员会毫无兴趣。他说，相

---

1 莫莉的英文是 Mollie。

education of the young was more important than anything that could be done for those who were already grown up. It happened that Jessie and Bluebell had both **whelped**① soon after the hay harvest, giving birth between them to nine sturdy puppies. As soon as they were **weaned**②, Napoleon took them away from their mothers, saying that he would make himself responsible for their education. He took them up into a **loft**③ which could only be reached by a ladder from the harness-room, and there kept them in such **seclusion**④ that the rest of the farm soon forgot their existence.

The mystery of where the milk went to was soon cleared up. It was mixed every day into the pigs' mash. The early apples were now ripening, and the grass of the orchard was littered with windfalls. The animals had assumed as a matter of course that these would be shared out equally; one day, however, the order went forth that all the windfalls were to be collected and brought to the harness-room for the use of the pigs. At this some of the other animals murmured, but it was no use. All the pigs were in full agreement on this point, even Snowball and Napoleon. Squealer was sent to make the necessary explanations to the others.

"Comrades!" he cried. "You do not imagine, I hope, that we pigs are doing this in a spirit of selfishness and privilege? Many of us actually dislike milk and apples. I dislike them myself. Our sole object in taking these things is to preserve our health. Milk and apples (this has been proved by Science, comrades) contain substances absolutely necessary to the well-being of a pig. We pigs are brainworkers. The whole management and organisation of this farm depend on us. Day and night we are watching over your welfare. It is for your sake that we drink that milk and eat those apples. Do you know what would happen if we pigs failed in our duty? Jones would come back! Yes, Jones would come back! Surely, comrades," cried Squealer almost pleadingly, skipping from side to side and whisking his tail, "surely there is no one among you who wants to see Jones come back?"

Now if there was one thing that the animals were completely certain of, it was that they did not want Jones back. When it was put to them in this light,

① whelp [hwelp] v. 下崽
（儿）
② wean [wi:n] v. 使（婴儿或
幼小动物）断奶

③ loft [lɔft] n. 阁楼
④ seclusion [si:'klu:ʒən] n. 隔
离，隔绝

较于对那些已经成年的动物所做的事情，对年轻动物的教育更加重要。碰巧的是，杰西和蓝铃在收割草料之后双双分娩产崽了，总共产了九头幼崽。幼崽刚一断奶，拿破仑便把他们从母亲身边带走，并且说，他要承担起对他们的教育责任。他把他们领到了一间阁楼，只能从挽具房用楼梯才能抵达。让他们同外界隔绝起来，农场上的其他动物很快便忘记了他们的存在。

牛奶的去处之谜很快就解开了。牛奶每天都给掺进了猪饲料里。早熟品种的苹果这时正在成熟，果园的草丛中散落着被风刮下的果子。动物们理所当然地认为，这些果实大家可以平分。然而，有一天，上面吩咐下来了，被风刮下来的果子要收集起来，送到挽具房去，供那些猪食用。对此，一些动物嘀咕了起来，但是，无济于事。在这一点上，所有猪的意见是一致的，连雪球和拿破仑都如此。他们派尖嗓子去给其他动物做解释。

"同志们啊！"他大声说，"我希望，你们不要认为，我们猪这样做是出于自私和享受特权，知道吗？我们许多猪都厌恶牛奶和苹果。我自己就厌恶这些东西。我们吃这些东西的唯一目的就是为了保持健康的体魄。牛奶和苹果（科学已经证明了这一点，同志们）含有猪要保持健康体魄所必需的物质。我们猪是脑力劳动者。本农场全部管理和组织工作全靠我们呢。我们日日夜夜在守望着你们的幸福。正是为了你们，我们喝了那些牛奶，吃了那些苹果。我们猪若是不能履行好自己的职责，你们知道会发生什么吗？琼斯会回来的！是啊，琼斯会回来的！毫无疑问，同志们，"尖嗓子大声说，几乎带着恳求的语气，身子左蹦右跳，尾巴摇来摇去，"毫无疑问，你们中没有哪位希望看到琼斯回来吧？"

是啊，动物们若是对哪一件事情心知肚明的话，那就是，他们都不想要让琼斯回来。当从这样一个视角把

they had no more to say. The importance of keeping the pigs in good health was all too obvious. So it was agreed without further argument that the milk and the **windfall**① apples (and also the main crop of apples when they ripened) should be reserved for the pigs alone.

① windfall ['windfɔ:l] *n.* 风吹落果

问题说给他们听后，他们便无话可说了。让猪保持健康的体魄，其重要性是再明确不过了。因此，他们无须继续争论便达成了一致意见，牛奶和被风刮落的苹果（还有等到苹果成熟了之后，主要的收成）应该留给猪单独享用。

Chapter IV

By the late summer the news of what had happened on Animal Farm had spread across half the county. Every day Snowball and Napoleon sent out flights of pigeons whose instructions were to **mingle with**① the animals on neighbouring farms, tell them the story of the Rebellion, and teach them the tune of *Beasts of England*.

Most of this time Mr. Jones had spent sitting in the **taproom**② of the Red Lion at Willingdon, complaining to anyone who would listen of the monstrous injustice he had suffered in being turned out of his property by a pack of good-for-nothing animals. The other farmers sympathised in principle, but they did not at first give him much help. At heart, each of them was secretly wondering whether he could not somehow turn Jones's misfortune to his own advantage. It was lucky that the owners of the two farms which **adjoined**③ Animal Farm were on permanently bad terms. One of them, which was named Foxwood, was a large, neglected, old-fashioned farm, much overgrown by woodland, with all its pastures worn out and its hedges in a disgraceful condition. Its owner, Mr. Pilkington, was an easy-going gentleman farmer who spent most of his time in fishing or hunting according to the season. The other farm, which was called Pinchfield, was smaller and better kept. Its owner was a Mr. Frederick, a tough, **shrewd**④ man, perpetually involved in lawsuits and with a name for driving hard bargains. These two disliked each other so much that it was difficult for

第四章

夏末，动物农场上发生的事情传遍了大半个郡。雪球和拿破仑每天都派出几批鸽子，吩咐他们混入附近农场的动物中间，告诉他们反抗运动的事情，教他们唱《英格兰的牲畜》。

这期间，琼斯先生大部分时间都消磨在威灵登的"红狮"酒吧里。他遭受到了不公正的对待，竟然被一群无用的动物赶出了自己的家园。只要有人愿意听，他就会不停地向人家倾诉这件荒唐透顶的事情。其他农场主原则上对他表达同情，但是，他们一开始并没有对他提供多少帮助。内心里，他们中的每一位都在暗暗地盘算着，自己能否在一定程度上把琼斯的不幸遭遇转变成自身的利益。幸运的是，同动物农场接壤的两座农场的主人素来交恶。其中的一座名为狐狸林。该农场规模很大，疏于管理，风格老旧，树木丛生，一片荒芜，牧场荒废了，树篱没有修剪，一派萧疏的景象。农场主皮尔金顿先生是位性情随和的乡绅，根据季节的变化，大部分时间用于钓鱼或者狩猎。另一座农场名叫窄地。规模更小，管理得更加理想。农场主弗里德里克先生是个蛮横而又精明的人，总是官司不断，因算计苛刻而出名。两位农场主相互厌恶，所以，二人很难达成一致的看法，即便是为了保护他们自身的利益。

① mingle with 和······混合
② taproom ['tæprum] *n.* 酒吧

③ adjoin [ə'dʒɔin] *v.* 与······毗连

④ shrewd [ʃru:d] *a.* 精明的

them to come to any agreement, even in defence of their own interests.

Nevertheless, they were both thoroughly frightened by the rebellion on Animal Farm, and very anxious to prevent their own animals from learning too much about it. At first they pretended to laugh to **scorn**① the idea of animals managing a farm for themselves. The whole thing would be over in a fortnight, they said. They put it about that the animals on the Manor Farm (they insisted on calling it the Manor Farm; they would not tolerate the name "Animal Farm") were perpetually fighting among themselves and were also rapidly starving to death. When time passed and the animals had evidently not starved to death, Frederick and Pilkington changed their tune and began to talk of the terrible **wickedness**② that now flourished on Animal Farm. It was given out that the animals there practised **cannibalism**③, tortured one another with red-hot horseshoes, and had their females in common. This was what came of rebelling against the laws of Nature, Frederick and Pilkington said.

However, these stories were never fully believed. Rumours of a wonderful farm, where the human beings had been turned out and the animals managed their own affairs, continued to circulate in vague and distorted forms, and throughout that year a wave of rebelliousness ran through the countryside. Bulls which had always been **tractable**④ suddenly turned **savage**⑤, sheep broke down hedges and **devoured**⑥ the clover, cows kicked the **pail**⑦ over, hunters refused their fences and shot their riders on to the other side. Above all, the tune and even the words of *Beasts of England* were known everywhere. It had spread with astonishing speed. The human beings could not contain their rage when they heard this song, though they pretended to think it merely ridiculous. They could not understand, they said, how even animals could bring themselves to sing such **contemptible**⑧ rubbish. Any animal caught singing it was given a **flogging**⑨ on the spot. And yet the song was **irrepressible**⑩. The blackbirds whistled it in the hedges, the pigeons cooed it in the **elms**⑪, it got into the **din**⑫ of the **smithies**⑬ and the tune of the church bells. And when the human beings listened to it, they secretly

尽管如此，动物农场爆发的反抗运动还是完完全全令他们两个人诚惶诚恐。他们忧心忡忡，急于防止他们农场上的动物得知太多关于这方面的消息。说到动物自己管理一座农场，刚开始时，他们假装嘲笑和蔑视这种想法。整个事件过上十天半个月也就过去了，他们这样说。他们逢人就说，庄园农场上的动物们（他们坚持称之为庄园农场，因为无法忍受动物农场这个名称）相互之间不断地打架斗殴，而且很快就会饿死了。过了一段时间，很显然，那些动物并没有饿死。这时候，弗里德里克和皮尔金顿改变了自己的说话腔调，开始说动物农场弥漫着一股可怕的邪气。他们已经把话放出去了，说那儿的动物之间盛行相互残食，用烧红的马蹄铁相互折磨，而且还实行配偶共有。这就是违背自然法则的结果，弗里德里克和皮尔金顿这么说。

不过，关于他们说的这些事情，谁也没有完全相信过。动物们纷纷传言，说在一座奇妙的农场上，人类被驱逐出去了，动物们自己管理自己的事务。这种传言还在持续扩散，或含糊不清，或走了样儿。那一年，一股反抗的浪潮席卷了整个地区。素来温顺的公牛们突然变得野性十足；绵羊冲破了树篱，狂吃苜蓿；奶牛踢翻了奶桶；参与狩猎的马匹拒绝越过围栏，把骑在背上的人甩到了围栏的另一侧。最重要的是，《英格兰的牲畜》的旋律甚至歌词传遍了四面八方。传播的速度令人惊诧不已。人类听见这首歌时，尽管假装认为歌曲荒诞可笑，但内心里其实窝着难以抑制的怒火。他们说，他们无法理解，怎么连动物都会堕落到唱响如此卑鄙的垃圾歌曲。因此，凡是被逮着唱这支歌的动物，都会当场挨鞭子抽。但即便如此，歌曲的传唱还是势不可当。黑鸟在树篱间鸣唱，鸽子在榆树上咕咕。歌声与铁匠铺的打铁声和教堂里的钟声融为一体了。当人类听见歌声时，他们不禁暗暗颤抖，从中听出了对他们自己未来命运的预言。

① scorn [skɔːn] v. 轻蔑，鄙视

② wickedness ['wikidnis] n. 邪恶
③ cannibalism ['kænibəlizəm] n. 同类相食

④ tractable ['træktəbl] a. 温顺的
⑤ savage ['sævidʒ] a. 未驯化的
⑥ devour [di'vauə] v. 吞食
⑦ pail [peil] n. 桶

⑧ contemptible [kən'temptəbl] a. 可鄙的
⑨ flogging ['flɔgiŋ] n. 鞭打
⑩ irrepressible [.iri'presəbl] a. 压抑不住的
⑪ elm [elm] n. 榆（树）
⑫ din [din] n. 吵闹声
⑬ smithy ['smiði] n. 铁匠铺

trembled, hearing in it a **prophecy**① of their future doom.

Early in October, when the corn was cut and **stacked**② and some of it was already threshed, a flight of pigeons came whirling through the air and **alighted**③ in the yard of Animal Farm in the wildest excitement. Jones and all his men, with half a dozen others from Foxwood and Pinchfield, had entered the five-barred gate and were coming up the cart-track that led to the farm. They were all carrying sticks, except Jones, who was marching ahead with a gun in his hands. Obviously they were going to attempt the recapture of the farm.

This had long been expected, and all preparations had been made. Snowball, who had studied an old book of Julius Caesar's campaigns which he had found in the farmhouse, was in charge of the defensive operations. He gave his orders quickly, and in a couple of minutes every animal was at his post.

As the human beings approached the farm buildings, Snowball launched his first attack. All the pigeons, to the number of thirty-five, flew to and fro over the men's heads and **muted**④ upon them from mid-air; and while the men were dealing with this, the geese, who had been hiding behind the hedge, rushed out and **pecked**⑤ viciously at the **calves**⑥ of their legs. However, this was only a light **skirmishing**⑦ **manoeuvre**⑧, intended to create a little disorder, and the men easily drove the geese off with their sticks. Snowball now launched his second line of attack. Muriel, Benjamin, and all the sheep, with Snowball at the head of them, rushed forward and **prodded**⑨ and butted the men from every side, while Benjamin turned around and lashed at them with his small hoofs. But once again the men, with their sticks and their **hobnailed**⑩ boots, were too strong for them; and suddenly, at a **squeal**⑪ from Snowball, which was the signal for retreat, all the animals turned and fled through the gateway into the yard.

The men gave a shout of triumph. They saw, as they imagined, their enemies in flight, and they rushed after them in disorder. This was just what Snowball had intended. As soon as they were well inside the yard, the three horses, the three cows, and the rest of the pigs, who had been lying **in ambush**⑫

① prophecy ['prɔfisi] *n.* 预言

② stack [stæk] *v.* 把……垛起

③ alight [əˈlait] *v.* 落在

④ mute [mu:t] *v.* （鸟）排泄

⑤ peck [pek] *v.* 啄

⑥ calf [kɑ:f] *n.* 小腿

⑦ skirmishing [ˈskə:miʃiŋ] *n.* 小冲突

⑧ manoeuvre [məˈnu:və] *n.* 策略

⑨ prod [prɔd] *v.* （用手指、棍棒等）刺

⑩ hobnailed [ˈhɔbneild] *a.* 钉有平头钉的

⑪ squeal [skwi:l] *n.* 长声尖叫

⑫ lay in ambush 埋伏

十月初，谷物收割完毕，堆成了垛，其中的一部分已经脱粒了。这时候，一群鸽子在空中盘旋着，飞落到了动物农场的院落里，情绪激动，无法抑制。琼斯和他的雇员，还有来自狐狸林和窄地两座农场的另外五六个人，进入了那扇五道闩大门，顺着通向农场的马车道前行。他们全都拿着棍棒，只有琼斯例外，他的手上拿着猎枪冲在前头。很显然，他们这是想要收复农场。

动物们早就料到会有这么一着，而且严阵以待。雪球仔细阅读了一本讲述尤利乌斯·凯撒[1]历次战役的书籍，书是他在农场主住宅里发现的，他负责防御工作。他很快下达了命令，几分钟之后，每一只动物都各就各位了。

当人类接近农场的窝棚区时，雪球发动了首次进攻。鸽子总数达到三十五只，他们在那些人的头顶飞来飞去，从半空中往他们身上排泄粪便。人们在招架着这一行动的当儿，藏匿在树篱中的鹅群冲了出来，恶狠狠地朝着他们的腿肚子上啄去。不过，这只是一场小规模的前奏战，目的是打乱对方的阵脚。那些人挥舞着棍棒，轻而易举便把鹅群赶跑了。雪球现在发动了第二线的进攻。雪球领着穆里尔、本杰明，还有全部绵羊向前冲，从四面八方朝敌人又是戳又是顶的。期间，本杰明转过身，用自己的小蹄子对着敌人猛踢。但是，人类有棍棒和钉了铁钉的靴子，动物再次招架不住了。突然间，随着雪球发出的一声尖叫——这是撤退的信号，所有动物全部转身，从门口逃进了院子。

那些人发出了胜利的欢呼声。他们以为动物这是败逃了，于是一窝蜂地追击他们。这正中雪球的下怀。一群人刚刚完全进入到了院子里，那三匹马，三头奶牛，还有其余那些猪——他们事先一直埋伏在牛棚里——突

1　凯撒（Julius Caesar, 公元前 100～44）是罗马统帅、政治家，与庞培、克拉苏结成"前三头同盟"，后击败庞培，成为罗马独裁者，被共和派贵族杀害，订定儒略历，著有《高卢战记》等。

in the **cowshed**①, suddenly emerged in their rear, cutting them off. Snowball now gave the signal for the charge. He himself dashed straight for Jones. Jones saw him coming, raised his gun and fired. The pellets scored bloody **streaks**② along Snowball's back, and a sheep dropped dead. Without halting for an instant, Snowball flung his fifteen **stone**③ against Jones's legs. Jones was hurled into a pile of dung and his gun flew out of his hands. But the most terrifying spectacle of all was Boxer, rearing up on his hind legs and striking out with his great iron-shod hoofs like a **stallion**④. His very first blow took a stable-lad from Foxwood on the **skull**⑤ and stretched him lifeless in the mud. At the sight, several men dropped their sticks and tried to run. Panic overtook them, and the next moment all the animals together were chasing them round and round the yard. They were **gored**⑥, kicked, bitten, trampled on. There was not an animal on the farm that did not **take vengeance on**⑦ them after his own fashion. Even the cat suddenly leapt off a roof onto a cowman's shoulders and sank her claws in his neck, at which he yelled horribly. At a moment when the opening was clear, the men were glad enough to rush out of the yard and make a **bolt**⑧ for the main road. And so within five minutes of their invasion they were in **ignominious**⑨ retreat by the same way as they had come, with a flock of geese hissing after them and pecking at their calves all the way.

All the men were gone except one. Back in the yard Boxer was pawing with his hoof at the stable-lad who lay face down in the mud, trying to turn him over. The boy did not stir.

"He is dead," said Boxer sorrowfully. "I had no intention of doing that. I forgot that I was wearing iron shoes. Who will believe that I did not do this on purpose?"

"No sentimentality, comrade!" cried Snowball from whose wounds the blood was still dripping. "War is war. The only good human being is a dead one."

"I have no wish to take life, not even human life," repeated Boxer, and his eyes were full of tears.

"Where is Mollie?" exclaimed somebody.

① cowshed ['kau,ʃed] *n.* 牛棚

② streak [striːk] *n.* 条纹

③ stone [stəun] *n.* 英石（英制重量单位，相当于 14 磅）

④ stallion ['stæljən] *n.*（成年）公马，种马

⑤ skull [skʌl] *n.* 脑袋

⑥ gore [gɔː] *v.* 用角（或獠牙）抵

⑦ take vengeance on 向……报仇（或报复）

⑧ bolt [bəult] *n.* 快跑，逃跑

⑨ ignominious [,ignəu'miniəs] *a.* 不光彩的

然出现在了他们身后，阻断了他们的退路。雪球此时发出了进攻的信号。他自己径直地冲向琼斯。琼斯看见他过来，举起枪开火了。子弹擦过雪球的背部，划出了几道血痕，一只绵羊却中弹身亡了。雪球没有片刻停顿，立刻把自己二百多磅的体重朝着琼斯的两条腿撞过去。琼斯被撞倒在一堆粪便上，他的猎枪也从手上飞出去了。但是，最惊心动魄的一幕是拳击手，他用两条后腿让身子立了起来，像一匹牡马似的用钉了铁掌的大蹄子朝外踢。他头一蹄子便踢在一位来自狐狸林农场的小马倌的脑袋上。小马倌直挺挺地倒在泥坑里，无声无息。见此情景，几个人扔下棍棒，拼命逃跑。他们被吓得不知所措，紧接着，所有动物追逐着他们在院里打转。动物一个劲儿地朝着他们用角抵，用蹄子踢，用嘴咬，用脚踩。农场上所有动物无不以自己的方式对他们报仇雪恨。连那只猫都从一个棚屋顶上跳到牧牛人的肩膀上，用爪子刺进他的脖子。牧牛人痛得惨叫了起来。人们趁着门口没有动物堵住的片刻，欣喜地冲出院落，朝着大路的方向逃窜。至此，人们的侵入行动还不到五分钟便结束了。他们很不光彩地顺着来时的路撤退，一群鹅在他们身后发着尖锐的嘘声，紧追不舍，一路啄着他们的腿肚子。

那些人除了一个之外全都离开了。拳击手返回到了院落里，用蹄子扒了扒脸朝下躺在泥坑里的小马倌，想要把他翻过身来，但小伙子一动不动。

"他已经死了，"拳击手说，表情悲伤，"我并没有要把他弄死的意思。我忘记自己装了铁掌。有谁会相信我不是有意这样做的呢？"

"用不着伤感啊，同志！"雪球大声说着，他的伤口还在滴着血呢。"战争就是战争。只有死人才是善良的人。"

"我不希望剥夺性命，即使是人类的生命。"拳击手重申着说，两眼噙满了泪水。

"莫莉在哪儿呢？"某只动物激动地大声说着。

Mollie in fact was missing. For a moment there was great alarm; it was feared that the men might have harmed her in some way, or even carried her off with them. In the end, however, she was found hiding in her stall with her head buried among the hay in the manger. She had taken to flight as soon as the gun went off. And when the others came back from looking for her, it was to find that the stable-lad, who in fact was only stunned, had already recovered and made off.

The animals had now reassembled in the wildest excitement, each recounting his own **exploits**[①] in the battle at the top of his voice. An **impromptu**[②] celebration of the victory was held immediately. The flag was run up and *Beasts of England* was sung a number of times, then the sheep who had been killed was given a solemn funeral, a **hawthorn**[③] bush being planted on her grave. At the graveside Snowball made a little speech, emphasising the need for all animals to be ready to die for Animal Farm if need be.

The animals decided unanimously to create a military decoration, "Animal Hero, First Class," which was **conferred**[④] there and then on Snowball and Boxer. It consisted of a brass medal (they were really some old horse-brasses which had been found in the harness-room), to be worn on Sundays and holidays. There was also "Animal Hero, Second Class," which was conferred **posthumously**[⑤] on the dead sheep.

There was much discussion as to what the battle should be called. In the end, it was named the Battle of the Cowshed, since that was where the ambush had been sprung. Mr. Jones's gun had been found lying in the mud, and it was known that there was a supply of **cartridges**[⑥] in the farmhouse. It was decided to set the gun up at the foot of the flagstaff, like a piece of **artillery**[⑦], and to fire it twice a year—once on October the twelfth, the anniversary of the Battle of the Cowshed, and once on Midsummer Day, the anniversary of the Rebellion.

莫莉确实不见了。一时间，出现了巨大的恐慌。动物们担心，那些人可能会以某种方式伤害到她，甚至会把她给掳走。不过，最后，大家发现她躲藏在自己的厩棚里，头埋在马槽的干草堆中。刚才枪声刚刚响起，她便撒腿跑了。别的动物寻找她返回来时，发现那位小马倌苏醒过来了，而且已经离开，他其实只是昏过去了。

动物们现在聚集在一块儿，情绪疯狂，激动不已。每只动物都在用自己最大的嗓门叙述着自己在战斗中的业绩。于是，他们立刻举行了未经准备的庆功会。旗帜升起来了，《英格兰的牲畜》唱了许多遍，然后，为那只阵亡的绵羊举行了庄严的葬礼，她的坟头上栽了一丛山楂树。雪球在墓地做了一番简短的演讲，强调全体动物必须在需要的时候为了捍卫动物农场随时准备献出生命。

动物们一致决定，拟设立一种军功勋章制度。"一级动物英雄"勋章当即便授予给了雪球和拳击手。勋章是一枚铜牌（实际上，那是他们在挽具房找到的一些古旧的马具铜质饰品），需要在星期天和假日佩戴。还有"二级动物英雄"勋章追授给了那头阵亡的绵羊。

关于这场战斗命名的问题，大家进行了热烈的讨论。最后决定命名为"牛棚之战"，因为伏兵就是在那儿向敌人发起进攻的。他们在那儿的泥坑里找到了琼斯先生的猎枪。大家都知道，那幢住宅里还存放了子弹。动物们决定把那管猎枪立在旗杆脚下，当作礼炮，每年鸣放两次——一次在10月12日"牛棚之战"纪念日，一次在施洗约翰节"反抗运动"纪念日。

① exploit [ik'splɔit] n. 功勋
② impromptu [im'prɔmptjuː] n. 无准备的

③ hawthorn ['hɔːθɔːn] n. 山楂树

④ confer [kən'fəː] v. 授予

⑤ posthumously ['pɔstjuməsli] ad. 于死后

⑥ cartridge ['kɑːtridʒ] n. 子弹

⑦ artillery [ɑːˈtiləri] n. 大炮

Chapter V

As winter drew on, Mollie became more and more troublesome. She was late for work every morning and excused herself by saying that she had overslept, and she complained of mysterious pains, although her appetite was excellent. On every kind of **pretext**① she would run away from work and go to the drinking pool, where she would stand foolishly gazing at her own reflection in the water. But there were also rumours of something more serious. One day, as Mollie strolled **blithely**② into the yard, flirting her long tail and chewing at a stalk of hay, Clover took her aside.

"Mollie," she said, "I have something very serious to say to you. This morning I saw you looking over the hedge that divides Animal Farm from Foxwood. One of Mr. Pilkington's men was standing on the other side of the hedge. And I was a long way away, but I am almost certain I saw this — he was talking to you and you were allowing him to stroke your nose. What does that mean, Mollie?"

"He didn't! I wasn't! It isn't true!" cried Mollie, beginning to **prance**③ about and paw the ground.

"Mollie! Look me in the face. Do you give me your word of honour that that man was not stroking your nose?"

"It isn't true!" repeated Mollie, but she could not look Clover in the face,

第五章

冬天临近了，莫莉越来越让大家心烦。她每天上午干活儿时都迟到，还替自己开脱说睡过头了。她还总是抱怨遭受了莫名其妙的痛苦，尽管她胃口非常好。她找各种各样的借口逃避干活儿，跑到饮水的池塘边，傻乎乎地伫立在水边，注视着水中自己的映像。但是，也有一些性质更为严重的传说。一天，莫莉忸怩作态地摆着自己的长尾巴，嘴里嚼着一根草料，信步进入院落。这时候，苜蓿把她拉到了一旁。

"莫莉，"苜蓿说，"我有很严肃的事情对你说。今天上午，我看见你站在动物农场与狐狸林分界的树篱处朝那边看。有位皮尔金顿的雇员站在树篱的另一边。我当时所处的位置很远，但我几乎可以肯定，我看见他朝你走来，你让他抚摸你的鼻子。这是什么意思啊，莫莉？"

"他没有抚摸！我也没有让他摸！这不符合事实！"莫莉大声说，一边开始蹦跶起来，用蹄子扒地。

"莫莉！看着我。你敢不敢以名誉担保，那个人没有抚摸你的鼻子？"

"这不符合事实！"莫莉重申着说，但是，她不敢正面看苜蓿。紧接着，她撒腿便跑，快速跑到田地里去了。

① pretext ['pri:tekst] n. 借口

② blithely [blaiðli] ad. 无忧无虑地

③ prance [prɑːns] v. （马）后足立地腾跃

and the next moment she took to her heels and galloped away into the field.

A thought struck Clover. Without saying anything to the others, she went to Mollie's stall and turned over the straw with her hoof. Hidden under the straw was a little pile of lump sugar and several bunches of ribbon of different colours.

Three days later Mollie disappeared. For some weeks nothing was known of her whereabouts, then the pigeons reported that they had seen her on the other side of Willingdon. She was between the **shafts**① of a smart dogcart painted red and black, which was standing outside a public-house. A fat red-faced man in check **breeches**② and **gaiters**③, who looked like a publican, was stroking her nose and feeding her with sugar. Her coat was newly clipped and she wore a scarlet ribbon round her forelock. She appeared to be enjoying herself, so the pigeons said. None of the animals ever mentioned Mollie again.

In January there came bitterly hard weather. The earth was like iron, and nothing could be done in the fields. Many meetings were held in the big barn, and the pigs occupied themselves with planning out the work of the coming season. It had come to be accepted that the pigs, who were **manifestly**④ cleverer than the other animals, should decide all questions of farm policy, though their decisions had to be **ratified**⑤ by a majority vote. This arrangement would have worked well enough if it had not been for the disputes between Snowball and Napoleon. These two disagreed at every point where disagreement was possible. If one of them suggested sowing a bigger **acreage**⑥ with **barley**⑦, the other was certain to demand a bigger acreage of oats, and if one of them said that such and such a field was just right for cabbages, the other would declare that it was useless for anything except roots. Each had his own following, and there were some violent debates. At the Meetings Snowball often won over the majority by his brilliant speeches, but Napoleon was better at **canvassing**⑧ support for himself in between times. He was especially successful with the sheep. Of late the sheep had taken to bleating "Four legs good, two legs bad" both in and **out of season**⑨, and they often interrupted the Meeting with this. It was noticed that they were especially liable to break into "Four legs good, two legs bad" at

苜蓿突然想到了什么。她没有对其他任何动物吭声，径自走到了莫莉的厩棚边，用蹄子把那些干草料翻了个个儿。草料下面藏匿着一小堆方糖，还有几束各种颜色的饰带。

三天过后，莫莉失踪了。几个星期时间里，谁也不知道她的下落。后来，那些鸽子报告说，他们看见她在威灵登的另一边。莫莉拉着一辆漆成红白相间的轻便马车，停在一家酒馆的外面。有个体形肥硕、脸色通红的男子穿着格子马裤，打着绑腿，看上去像个酒馆老板。他正抚摸着莫莉的鼻子，喂糖块给她吃。她的皮毛是新近修剪过的，额毛处系着一根红色饰带。她显得自得其乐，鸽子们这样说。动物中谁也没有再提到过莫莉。

一月，恶劣难熬的天气到来了。土地像铁一般梆硬，田地里什么活儿也干不成。大谷仓里举行过许许多多次会议。那些猪集中注意力部署接下来一个季度的工作，动物们也已经接受了这样的事实，即猪明显比别的动物更加聪颖睿智，他们理应对事关农场政策的所有问题做出决定，虽说他们的决定需要得到绝大多数动物的赞成。如若不是因为雪球和拿破仑之间的分歧，这样的安排本来是能够行之有效的。但凡遇到可能产生分歧的事情，他们两位之间都产生分歧。他们中若是有一方建议扩大大麦的播种面积，另一方就肯定会要求扩大燕麦的播种面积。若是一方说某一块田里最适合于栽种白菜，另一方就会声称栽种什么都不成，只能栽种根茎作物。他们各有自己的支持者，双方会展开激烈的争论。各种"会议"上，雪球凭着自己雄辩的口才，往往能够赢得大多数动物的支持。但是，拿破仑善于休会期间的游说，替自己争取支持者。他在绵羊那儿取得了特别大的成功。最近，绵羊们喜欢咩咩地念叨着"四条腿好，两条腿坏"，在哪儿都这样，不管是否合乎时宜。他们常常这样念叨着，打断"会议"。大家注意到，但凡遇

① shaft [ʃɑːft] n. 辕杆
② breech [briːtʃ] n. 屁股
③ gaiter ['geitə] n. 绑腿

④ manifestly ['mænifestli] ad. 显然地

⑤ ratify ['rætifai] v. 认可

⑥ acreage ['eikəridʒ] n. 面积，英亩数
⑦ barley ['bɑːli] n. 大麦

⑧ canvass ['kænvəs] v. 拉选票
⑨ in / out of season 合宜的 / 不合时宜

crucial moments in Snowball's speeches. Snowball had made a close study of some **back numbers**[1] of the Farmer and Stockbreeder which he had found in the farmhouse, and was full of plans for innovations and improvements. He talked learnedly about field **drains**[2], **silage**[3], and basic **slag**[4], and had worked out a complicated scheme for all the animals to drop their dung directly in the fields, at a different spot every day, to save the labour of **cartage**[5]. Napoleon produced no schemes of his own, but said quietly that Snowball's would come to nothing, and seemed to be **biding his time**[6]. But of all their controversies, none was so bitter as the one that took place over the windmill.

In the long pasture, not far from the farm buildings, there was a small **knoll**[7] which was the highest point on the farm. After surveying the ground, Snowball declared that this was just the place for a windmill, which could be made to operate a **dynamo**[8] and supply the farm with electrical power. This would light the stalls and warm them in winter, and would also run a circular **saw**[9], a chaff-cutter, a mangel-slicer, and an electric milking machine. The animals had never heard of anything of this kind before (for the farm was an old-fashioned one and had only the most primitive machinery), and they listened in astonishment while Snowball **conjured up**[10] pictures of fantastic machines which would do their work for them while they grazed at their ease in the fields or improved their minds with reading and conversation.

Within a few weeks Snowball's plans for the windmill were fully worked out. The mechanical details came mostly from three books which had belonged to Mr. Jones — *One Thousand Useful Things to Do About the House, Every Man His Own Bricklayer,* and *Electricity for Beginners.* Snowball used as his study a shed which had once been used for **incubators**[11] and had a smooth wooden floor, suitable for drawing on. He was **closeted**[12] there for hours at a time. With his books held open by a stone, and with a piece of chalk **gripped**[13] between the knuckles of his trotter, he would move rapidly to and fro, drawing in line after line and uttering little **whimpers**[14] of excitement. Gradually the plans grew into a complicated mass of cranks and cog-wheels, covering more than half the floor,

到雪球演讲的关键时刻，他们就会念叨起"四条腿好，两条腿坏"。雪球在农场主的住宅里找到了几本《农场主与畜牧业者》杂志的过刊。他对其进行了仔细的阅读，于是，脑袋里尽装着革新和改进的计划。他有理有据，谈到了田地灌溉、饲料保鲜、碱性炉渣处理等等。他制定出了一套复杂的计划，让所有动物每天在不同地点直接把粪便排入田地，以便节省用大车运送的劳动量。拿破仑自己没有制定出什么计划，但态度平静地说，雪球的计划会毫无结果。他好像在等待时机。但是，他们之间的分歧最严重的莫过于围绕风车一事。

离农场窝棚区不远的那片长长的牧场上，有一个小山包，那是农场的最高点。雪球勘察了地形后宣布，那是设置风车的最佳地点。风车可以用来发电，给农场提供电能。这样可以给厩棚提供照明，冬季里给厩棚保温，另外，还可以带动一台圆锯机床、一台割草机、一台甜菜切片机以及一台电动挤奶机。动物们过去压根儿就没有听说过有这样的东西（因为这座农场是旧式风格的，只有那些老掉牙的机械设备）。那些奇妙的机器会替动物们干活儿，而他们则悠然自得在田地里吃着草，或者阅读交谈，长才益智。雪球描绘着关于机器的一幅幅图画，他们听得目瞪口呆。

不出几个星期，雪球关于建造风车的方案完全制定出来了。具体的机械图形取自属于琼斯先生的三本书——《房屋建造大全》《人人都是泥水工》和《电工入门》。雪球把一间曾经用来存放孵化器的窝棚用作自己的书房，铺上了光滑的木地板，适合在上面绘制图纸。他把自己关在房间里，一待就是几个小时。他用石头压着翻开的书本，蹄子趾间夹着一支粉笔，快速地来回移动，画出一根又一根线条，一边还激动地小声哼哼。他绘制的图慢慢地演变成了一大堆复杂的曲轴和齿轮图案，占据了一半地板的面积。对于这些东西，其他动物完全看得云里雾里，但却惊叹不已。所有动

① back numbers 过期刊物

② drain [drein] *n.* 排水管

③ silage ['sailidʒ] *n.* 青贮饲料

④ slag [slæg] *n.* 炉渣

⑤ cartage ['kɑːtidʒ] *n.* 运输

⑥ bide one's time 等待时机

⑦ knoll [nəul] *n.* 圆丘

⑧ dynamo ['dainəməu] *n.* 电动机

⑨ saw [sɔː] *n.* 锯子

⑩ conjure up 用魔法召唤

⑪ incubator ['inkjubeitə] *n.* 孵化器

⑫ closet ['klɔzit] *v.* 把（自己）关在私室里与人密谈

⑬ grip [grip] *v.* 握住

⑭ whimper ['hwimpə] *n.* 呜咽声

which the other animals found completely **unintelligible**① but very impressive. All of them came to look at Snowball's drawings at least once a day. Even the hens and ducks came, and were **at pains**② not to tread on the chalk marks. Only Napoleon held aloof. He had declared himself against the windmill from the start. One day, however, he arrived unexpectedly to examine the plans. He walked heavily round the shed, looked closely at every detail of the plans and snuffed at them once or twice, then stood for a little while contemplating them out of the corner of his eye; then suddenly he lifted his leg, **urinated**③ over the plans, and walked out without uttering a word.

The whole farm was deeply divided on the subject of the windmill. Snowball did not deny that to build it would be a difficult business. Stone would have to be carried and built up into walls, then the **sails**④ would have to be made and after that there would be need for dynamos and cables. (How these were to be **procured**⑤, Snowball did not say.) But he maintained that it could all be done in a year. And thereafter, he declared, so much labour would be saved that the animals would only need to work three days a week. Napoleon, on the other hand, argued that the great need of the moment was to increase food production, and that if they wasted time on the windmill they would all starve to death. The animals formed themselves into two factions under the slogan, "Vote for Snowball and the three-day week" and "Vote for Napoleon and the full manger." Benjamin was the only animal who did not side with either faction. He refused to believe either that food would become more plentiful or that the windmill would save work. Windmill or no windmill, he said, life would go on as it had always gone on—that is, badly.

Apart from the disputes over the windmill, there was the question of the defence of the farm. It was fully realised that though the human beings had been defeated in the Battle of the Cowshed they might make another and more determined attempt to recapture the farm and **reinstate**⑥ Mr. Jones. They had all the more reason for doing so because the news of their defeat had spread across the countryside and made the animals on the neighbouring farms more **restive**⑦

① unintelligible
[ˌʌnin'telidʒəbl] *a.* 难理解的

② at pains 尽力；用心

③ urinate ['juərineit] *v.* 小便

④ sail [seil] *n.*（风车等的）翼板

⑤ procure [prəu'kjuə] *v.* 获得，取得

⑥ reinstate [ˌri:in'steit] *v.* 使复工

⑦ restive ['restiv] *a.* 难驾驭的

物每天都至少要来看一次雪球绘制的图形。连母鸡和鸭子都来了，而且铆足了劲，尽量不让自己踩踏到那些粉笔画出的线条。只有拿破仑心高气傲，不屑一顾。他从一开始就公开表示反对建造风车。不过，有一天，他出乎意料地来观看图形。他迈着沉重的脚步在窝棚内打转，仔细查看图形的每一处细节，有一两次还用鼻孔闻了闻，然后伫立片刻，斜睨着眼睛看。紧接着，他突然抬起一条腿，在图上面撒了一泡尿，没吭一声便出去了。

有关风车一事，整座农场陷入了严重的分裂状态。雪球并不否认，建造风车是一件很艰难的事情。需要运来石头，垒成墙壁，然后还要制作风车的翼板，随后还需要发电机和电缆线。（这些东西如何实现，雪球没有说。）但是，他坚持说，一年之内便可完成。那之后，他声称，劳动量便可以大大减少，动物们每个星期只需要工作三天。相反，拿破仑认为，眼下迫切需要的是增加饲料的生产。倘若他们把时间浪费在建造风车上面，他们都会饿死。动物们在不同口号下组成了两个阵营。一方的口号是"支持雪球和三天工作制"，另一方的口号是"支持拿破仑和食料满槽"。本杰明是唯一保持中立的动物。他既不相信会饲料富足，也不相信风车能够节省劳力。他说，有没有风车，生活还是会一如既往地进行下去——那就是，过得很糟糕。

除了围绕风车产生分歧之外，还有农场防御的问题。动物们充分地意识到，虽说人类在"牛棚之战"中吃了败仗，但是，他们可能态度坚决，一而再再而三地企图重新占领农场，让琼斯先生复职。他们有更加充分的理由这样做，因为他们战败的消息传遍了整个地区，让临近农场的动物们比以往任何时候都更加桀骜不驯了。和往常一样，雪球与拿破仑还是达不成一致意见。根据拿破仑的意见，动物们一定要设法搞到武器，并且训练他们使用武器。根据雪球的意见，

than ever. As usual, Snowball and Napoleon were in disagreement. According to Napoleon, what the animals must do was to procure firearms and train themselves in the use of them. According to Snowball, they must send out more and more pigeons and **stir up**① rebellion among the animals on the other farms. The one argued that if they could not defend themselves they were bound to be conquered, the other argued that if rebellions happened everywhere they would have no need to defend themselves. The animals listened first to Napoleon, then to Snowball, and could not make up their minds which was right; indeed, they always found themselves in agreement with the one who was speaking at the moment.

At last the day came when Snowball's plans were completed. At the Meeting on the following Sunday the question of whether or not to begin work on the windmill was to be put to the vote. When the animals had assembled in the big barn, Snowball stood up and, though occasionally interrupted by bleating from the sheep, set forth his reasons for advocating the building of the windmill. Then Napoleon stood up to reply. He said very quietly that the windmill was nonsense and that he advised nobody to vote for it, and promptly sat down again; he had spoken for barely thirty seconds, and seemed almost indifferent as to the effect he produced. At this Snowball sprang to his feet, and shouting down the sheep, who had begun bleating again, broke into a passionate appeal in favour of the windmill. Until now the animals had been about equally divided in their sympathies, but in a moment Snowball's **eloquence**② had carried them away. In **glowing**③ sentences he painted a picture of Animal Farm as it might be when **sordid**④ labour was lifted from the animals' backs. His imagination had now run far beyond chaff-cutters and turnip-slicers. Electricity, he said, could operate threshing machines, ploughs, harrows, rollers, and reapers and binders, besides supplying every stall with its own electric light, hot and cold water, and an electric heater. By the time he had finished speaking, there was no doubt as to which way the vote would go. But just at this moment Napoleon stood up and, casting a peculiar **sidelong**⑤ look at Snowball, uttered a high-pitched whimper of a kind no one had ever heard him utter before.

① stir up 激起

他们要把越来越多的鸽子放出去，到别的农场上去煽动动物们起来反抗。一方认为，他们若是不能自我防卫，那注定会被征服。另一方则认为，如若四处爆发反抗运动，他们便无须自我防卫。动物们先听了拿破仑的看法，然后又听雪球的，莫衷一是，打不定主意。事实上，他们往往会发现，听哪个说，就会觉得哪个说得有道理。

最后，雪球的设计图终于完成了。随后那个星期天的"会议"上，大家拟对是否开工建造风车进行表决。动物们在大谷仓集中后，雪球站立起来，尽管时不时地被绵羊咩咩的声音打断，但还是仔细地陈述了力主建造风车的理由。紧接着，拿破仑站起来反击。他态度平静地说，建造风车的事情纯属瞎胡闹，奉劝大家都不要对其投赞成票，但立刻又坐下来了。他的讲话仅仅持续了三十秒而已，好像并不关注自己的讲话取得了什么样的效果。听到拿破仑这么一说后，雪球立刻一跃身子站了起来，先朝下对着那些绵羊吼了一通，因为他们又开始咩咩叫起来了，然后情绪激动地恳求大家支持建造风车。至此，动物中两个阵营旗鼓相当，势均力敌，但是，片刻之后，雪球雄辩的演讲征服了他们。动物农场上繁重的体力劳动从动物们的肩膀上卸去之后，将会是一幅

② eloquence ['eləkwəns] *n.* 雄辩
③ glowing ['gləuiŋ] *a.* 生动的
④ sordid ['sɔːdid] *a.* 悲惨的

怎么样的图画，他用生动形象的语言进行了描绘。他的想象力此刻远远超出了割草机和萝卜切片机的范围。他说，电力除了让每一间厩棚拥有自身的照明、热水、冷水以及电热器之外，还可以发动脱粒机、犁、耙、碾子、收割机以及捆草机。等到雪球演讲完毕时，动物们该把赞成票投给谁，已经不存在疑问了。但是，也就在这个当儿，拿破仑站起身来，斜着眼睛瞥了雪球一眼，目光显得特别，并发出了一声尖叫，动物们过去从来都没有听见从他嘴里发出过这样的叫声。

⑤ sidelong ['saidlɔŋ] *a.* 侧面的

At this there was a terrible baying sound outside, and nine enormous dogs wearing brass-studded **collars**① came bounding into the barn. They dashed straight for Snowball, who only sprang from his place just in time to escape their snapping jaws. In a moment he was out of the door and they were after him. Too amazed and frightened to speak, all the animals crowded through the door to watch the chase. Snowball was racing across the long pasture that led to the road. He was running as only a pig can run, but the dogs were close **on his heels**②. Suddenly he slipped and it seemed certain that they had him. Then he was up again, running faster than ever, then the dogs were gaining on him again. One of them all but closed his jaws on Snowball's tail, but Snowball **whisked**③ it free just in time. Then he put on an extra **spurt**④ and, with a few inches to spare, slipped through a hole in the hedge and was seen no more.

Silent and terrified, the animals crept back into the barn. In a moment the dogs came bounding back. At first no one had been able to imagine where these creatures came from, but the problem was soon solved: they were the puppies whom Napoleon had taken away from their mothers and reared privately. Though not yet full-grown, they were huge dogs, and as fierce-looking as wolves. They kept close to Napoleon. It was noticed that they **wagged**⑤ their tails to him in the same way as the other dogs had been used to do to Mr. Jones.

Napoleon, with the dogs following him, now mounted on to the raised portion of the floor where Major had previously stood to deliver his speech. He announced that from now on the Sunday morning Meetings would come to an end. They were unnecessary, he said, and wasted time. In future all questions relating to the working of the farm would be settled by a special committee of pigs, presided over by himself. These would meet in private and afterwards communicate their decisions to the others. The animals would still assemble on Sunday mornings to **salute**⑥ the flag, sing *Beasts of England*, and receive their orders for the week; but there would be no more debates.

In spite of the shock that Snowball's expulsion had given them, the animals were **dismayed**⑦ by this announcement. Several of them would have protested

① collar ['kɔlə] *n.* 颈圈

② on one's heels 紧追某人

③ whisk [hwisk] *v.* 飞快地掠过

④ spurt [spəːt] *n.* 冲刺

⑤ wag [wæg] *v.* 摇动

⑥ salute [sə'ljuːt] *v.* 升旗向……致意

⑦ dismay [dis'mei] *v.* 使灰心丧气

这一声尖叫过后，会场外面响起了一阵恐怖的狂吠声，九条戴着铜饰项圈的体大身长的狗蹦蹦跳着冲进了大谷仓。他们径直地扑向雪球，雪球及时一跃身子离开了原地，这才躲避开了狗的尖齿利牙。片刻之后，雪球到了门外，他们追在他身后。所有动物都异常惊愕惶恐，说不出话来，全都涌到门口外面，观看这场追逐之战。雪球跑过那片延伸到大路边的长条形牧场。他跑得再快也不能超出猪奔跑的速度，但那些狗还是紧追不舍。突然间，他滑倒了，看起来他们肯定要逮着他了。紧接着，他爬了起来，比先前跑得更快了，那些狗再次赶上了他。其中的一条几乎都咬住雪球的尾巴了，但雪球还是及时甩脱了。随后，雪球竭尽全力冲刺，和狗的距离就差那么几英寸，终于从树篱间的一个缺口处溜了出去，不见了踪影。

动物们沉默不语，战战兢兢，一个个爬回了谷仓。转眼间，那些狗蹦跳着回来了。开始时，谁也想象不到，这些畜生来自何方，但是，问题很快就有了答案。原来他们打小便由拿破仑从他们的母亲身边领走，独自饲养长大。虽说还没有完全成年，但已经够体大身长了，外形像狼一样凶狠。他们紧紧跟随在拿破仑身边。大家注意到，如同别的狗对着琼斯先生摇尾巴一样，他们也对着拿破仑摇尾巴。

拿破仑此时登上了先前少校站在上面发表演讲的那个隆起的台子，身后跟随着那些狗。他宣布，从现在开始，星期天上午不再举行"会议"了。他说，这样的会议没有必要，浪费时间。今后，凡是涉及农场运作的问题都由猪组成的特别委员会来解决。该特别委员会由他本人担任主席。这样的会议将秘密举行，然后再把决定通报给其他动物。动物们仍然在星期日上午聚会，向旗帜致敬，唱《英格兰的牲畜》，接受他们下一个星期的工作任务，但不会再有争论了。

尽管动物们因雪球遭到狗的驱赶感到震惊，但刚才

if they could have found the right arguments. Even Boxer was vaguely troubled. He set his ears back, shook his forelock several times, and tried hard to **marshal**① his thoughts; but in the end he could not think of anything to say. Some of the pigs themselves, however, were more articulate. Four young porkers in the front row uttered shrill squeals of disapproval, and all four of them sprang to their feet and began speaking at once. But suddenly the dogs sitting round Napoleon let out deep, **menacing**② **growls**③, and the pigs fell silent and sat down again. Then the sheep broke out into a tremendous bleating of "Four legs good, two legs bad!" which went on for nearly a quarter of an hour and put an end to any chance of discussion.

Afterwards Squealer was sent round the farm to explain the new arrangement to the others.

"Comrades," he said, "I trust that every animal here appreciates the sacrifice that Comrade Napoleon has made in taking this extra labour upon himself. Do not imagine, comrades, that leadership is a pleasure! On the contrary, it is a deep and heavy responsibility. No one believes more firmly than Comrade Napoleon that all animals are equal. He would be only too happy to let you make your decisions for yourselves. But sometimes you might make the wrong decisions, comrades, and then where should we be? Suppose you had decided to follow Snowball, with his moonshine of windmills—Snowball, who, as we now know, was no better than a criminal?"

"He fought bravely at the Battle of the Cowshed," said somebody.

"Bravery is not enough," said Squealer. "Loyalty and obedience are more important. And as to the Battle of the Cowshed, I believe the time will come when we shall find that Snowball's part in it was much exaggerated. Discipline, comrades, iron discipline! That is the **watchword**④ for today. One false step, and our enemies would be upon us. Surely, comrades, you do not want Jones back?"

Once again this argument was unanswerable. Certainly the animals did not

① marshal ['mɑːʃəl] *v.* 整理

② menacing ['menəsiŋ] *a.* 恐吓的
③ growl [graul] *n.* 低鸣声

④ watchword ['wɔtʃwəːd] *n.* 口令

宣布的这个决定更是令他们沮丧不已。其中有几只动物本想提出抗议，但苦于没有找到正当的理由。连拳击手都隐隐地感到不安起来。他耳朵朝后竖着，几次抖动额毛，设法理清自己的思路，但到头来，他还是想不出要说什么。不过，有几头猪倒是更有表达能力的。前排的四只小肥猪发出尖叫，表达自己的不满，四头猪全部都跳跃起来，同时说话。但突然间，围坐在拿破仑身边的那些狗发出低沉带有威胁的长吠，几头猪缄口不言了，重新坐了下来。紧接着，绵羊们突然大声咩咩地说出"四条腿好，两条腿坏！"咩咩声持续了一刻钟之久，任何继续讨论的可能性都成了泡影。

过后，尖嗓子被派到农场各处去向其他动物解释这种新的安排。

"同志们，"尖嗓子说，"拿破仑同志自己承担起这项额外的工作，我相信，这里的每一只动物都欣赏他的这种牺牲精神。同志们啊，不要以为，担任领导是一件很舒心惬意的事情！恰恰相反，这是一种深刻而又重大的责任。拿破仑同志相信，一切动物都是平等的。比较起来，任何动物的信念都没有他的坚定。他本来很愿意你们自己替自己做主的，但是，你们有时候可能会做出错误的决断，同志们，这样一来，我们的处境会如何呢？假定你们刚才决定跟随雪球，相信他那套关于风车的空谈——雪球是什么人？我们大家都知道，比罪犯好不到哪儿去！"

"他在'牛棚之战'中英勇战斗。"某只动物说。

"只凭英勇不够啊，"尖嗓子说，"忠诚与服从更加重要。至于'牛棚之战'，我们将会发现，雪球在战斗中的作用被严重夸大了。我相信，这样的时候会到来的。纪律，同志们，铁的纪律！这是我们今天的口号。走错一步，我们的敌人就会向我们反扑。毫无疑问，同志们，你们不想要琼斯回来对吧？"

这个理由再次无可辩驳。当然，动物们不想看到琼

want Jones back; if the holding of debates on Sunday mornings was liable to bring him back, then the debates must stop. Boxer, who had now had time to think things over, voiced the general feeling by saying: "If Comrade Napoleon says it, it must be right." And from then on he adopted the maxim, "Napoleon is always right," in addition to his private motto of "I will work harder."

By this time the weather had broken and the spring ploughing had begun. The shed where Snowball had drawn his plans of the windmill had been shut up and it was assumed that the plans had been rubbed off the floor. Every Sunday morning at ten o'clock the animals assembled in the big barn to receive their orders for the week. The **skull**[1] of old Major, now clean of flesh, had been **disinterred**[2] from the orchard and set up on a **stump**[3] at the foot of the flagstaff, beside the gun. After the hoisting of the flag, the animals were required to file past the skull in a reverent manner before entering the barn. Nowadays they did not sit all together as they had done in the past. Napoleon, with Squealer and another pig named Minimus, who had a remarkable gift for composing songs and poems, sat on the front of the raised platform, with the nine young dogs forming a **semicircle**[4] round them, and the other pigs sitting behind. The rest of the animals sat facing them in the main body of the barn. Napoleon read out the orders for the week in a **gruff**[5] soldierly style, and after a single singing of *Beasts of England*, all the animals **dispersed**[6].

On the third Sunday after Snowball's expulsion, the animals were somewhat surprised to hear Napoleon announce that the windmill was to be built after all. He did not give any reason for having changed his mind, but merely warned the animals that this extra task would mean very hard work, it might even be necessary to reduce their rations. The plans, however, had all been prepared, down to the last detail. A special committee of pigs had been at work upon them for the past three weeks. The building of the windmill, with various other improvements, was expected to take two years.

That evening Squealer explained privately to the other animals that Napoleon had never in reality been opposed to the windmill. On the contrary, it

斯回来。倘若星期日上午的争论有导致他回来的危险，那么，争论必须停止。拳击手现在有时间把一桩桩事情考虑清楚。他表达了大家的心声，说，"既然拿破仑同志都这样说，那就一定是对的。"从此刻开始，他把"拿破仑总是对的"当作格言，作为他自己的座右铭"我要更加卖力干活儿"的补充。

到了这时候，天气突然向好，春耕开始了。当初雪球用于绘制风车蓝图的那间棚屋一直关闭着。动物们认为，地板上的那些图形已经被擦掉了。每个星期天的上午，动物们都聚集在大谷仓内，接受下一星期他们要承担的工作任务。老少校的头盖骨现在已经没有了肉。动物们把它从果园里挖了出来，陈列在旗杆下那管猎枪旁边的一个树桩上。升旗仪式结束之后，动物们要按照要求，态度毕恭毕敬，列队从少校的头盖骨旁边走过，然后进入大谷仓。现如今，他们不再像往昔一样，所有动物坐在一块儿。拿破仑和尖嗓子以及另外一头名叫小不点的猪——小不点具备不同凡响的天赋，会作曲赋诗——坐在隆起的台子上，那九条年轻的狗绕着他们围成了个半圆，其他猪则坐在后面。其他动物面对他们坐着，占据了谷仓的大部分空间。拿破仑以粗犷的军人作风宣读一个星期工作安排的命令。动物们唱过《英格兰的牲畜》之后便四散开了。

雪球遭到驱逐后的第三个星期天，拿破仑宣布，农场上还是打算要建造风车。动物们听后多少还是感到有点吃惊。拿破仑没有说明自己改变主意的缘由，而仅仅是提醒动物们，这份额外的工作任务需要大家吃大苦，甚至有可能要紧缩他们的饲料配额。不过，设计工作已经准备好了，周密到了最后一个细节。由猪组成的一个特别委员会已经为这件事情工作了三个星期。建造风车和其他各项改进工程预计花费两年时间。

当晚，尖嗓子私下里对其他动物解释说，拿破仑事实上从来都不反对建造风车。恰恰相反，当初正是他力

① skull [skʌl] *n.* 头骨
② disinter [ˌdisin'tɜː] *v.* 挖出
③ stump [stʌmp] *n.* 树桩
④ semicircle ['semiˌsɜːkl] *n.* 半圆
⑤ gruff [grʌf] *a.* 低沉沙哑的
⑥ disperse [dis'pɜːs] *v.* 解散

was he who had advocated it in the beginning, and the plan which Snowball had drawn on the floor of the incubator shed had actually been stolen from among Napoleon's papers. The windmill was, in fact, Napoleon's own creation. Why, then, asked somebody, had he spoken so strongly against it? Here Squealer looked very **sly**[①]. That, he said, was Comrade Napoleon's **cunning**[②]. He had seemed to oppose the windmill, simply as a manoeuvre to get rid of Snowball, who was a dangerous character and a bad influence. Now that Snowball was out of the way, the plan could go forward without his interference. This, said Squealer, was something called **tactics**[③]. He repeated a number of times, "Tactics, comrades, tactics!" skipping round and whisking his tail with a merry laugh. The animals were not certain what the word meant, but Squealer spoke so persuasively, and the three dogs who happened to be with him growled so threateningly, that they accepted his explanation without further questions.

主这件事的。雪球在存放孵化器那间棚屋的地板上绘制的图形实际上是从拿破仑的文件中盗取的。风车事实上是拿破仑的个人创造。这时候，有只动物问，他当初为什么那么强烈反对建造风车呢？面对这个问题，尖嗓子显得神情诡秘。他说，这正是拿破仑同志智慧的体现。他当时表面上反对建造风车，那只是一个清除雪球的策略，因为雪球是个危险的主儿，影响恶劣。雪球既然已经被清除掉了，那么，该计划便可以推进实施，而不至于受到他的干扰。尖嗓子说，这种事情叫作策略。他重复说了好几遍："策略，同志们，策略啊！"身子蹦跶着转圈儿，不停地摇着尾巴，兴致勃勃地哈哈大笑起来。动物们对这个词的含义心里没有底，但是，尖嗓子的说辞很有说服力，加上正好同他待在一块儿的三条狗狂吠了起来，充满了威慑力，动物们便认同了他的解释，不再提出质疑了。

① sly [slai] *a.* 狡猾的
② cunning ['kʌniŋ] *n.* 狡诈

③ tactic ['tæktik] *n.* 策略

Chapter VI

All that year the animals worked like slaves. But they were happy in their work; they **grudged**① no effort or sacrifice, well aware that everything that they did was for the benefit of themselves and those of their kind who would come after them, and not for a pack of idle, thieving human beings.

Throughout the spring and summer they worked a sixty-hour week, and in August Napoleon announced that there would be work on Sunday afternoons as well. This work was strictly voluntary, but any animal who absented himself from it would have his rations reduced by half. Even so, it was found necessary to leave certain tasks undone. The harvest was a little less successful than in the previous year, and two fields which should have been sown with roots in the early summer were not sown because the ploughing had not been completed early enough. It was possible to foresee that the coming winter would be a hard one.

The windmill presented unexpected difficulties. There was a good **quarry**② of limestone on the farm, and plenty of sand and cement had been found in one of the outhouses, so that all the materials for building were at hand. But the problem the animals could not at first solve was how to break up the stone into pieces of suitable size. There seemed no way of doing this except with **picks**③ and **crowbars**④, which no animal could use, because no animal could

第六章

① grudge [grʌdʒ] v. 吝惜

整个一年期间，动物们像奴隶一样干着活儿。但是，他们干得很快乐，不偷懒，不怕牺牲，心里很清楚，他们所做的一切都是为了自己的福祉，还有他们后代的福祉，而不是为了那帮游手好闲、偷盗成性的人类。

整个春夏两季，他们实行每星期六十小时工作制。到了八月，拿破仑宣布，星期天下午也得干活儿。这种额外的活儿严格实行自愿原则，但是，若是有动物缺席了，那他的饲料配额就得减半。即便如此，大家发现，有些工作任务还是完不成。比较上一年，当年的收割显得有些逊色。有两片地本来初夏是应该种植根菜植物的，但因为没有尽早耕耘而未能种上。可以预料得到，即将到来的冬季将会很艰难。

② quarry ['kwɔri] n. 采石场

建造风车的工程出现了始料未及的困难。农场里有一处高质量的采石场，同时，动物们在一间棚屋里还发现存有大量沙子和水泥，建筑材料都是现成的。但是，动物们开始就遇到了无法解决的问题，即不知道如何将石料破开，形成大小适中的小块。这项工作看起来只能使用镐和撬棍，否则无法进行。而动物们

③ pick [pik] n. 镐
④ crowbar ['krəu,bɑː] n. 撬棍

偏偏又不会使用那些工具，因为任何动物都不能用后腿站立。白费了几个星期的力气之后，才有动物想出了好办法，即利用地心力的作用。采石场处处都是巨

stand on his hind legs. Only after weeks of vain effort did the right idea occur to somebody namely to **utilise**^① the force of gravity. Huge **boulders**^②, far too big to be used as they were, were lying all over the bed of the quarry. The animals lashed ropes round these, and then all together, cows, horses, sheep, any animal that could lay hold of the rope—even the pigs sometimes joined in at critical moments—they dragged them with desperate slowness up the slope to the top of the quarry, where they were **toppled**^③ over the edge, to shatter to pieces below. Transporting the stone when it was once broken was comparatively simple. The horses carried it off in cart-loads, the sheep dragged single blocks, even Muriel and Benjamin **yoked**^④ themselves into an old governess-cart and did their share. By late summer a sufficient store of stone had accumulated, and then the building began, under the **superintendence**^⑤ of the pigs.

But it was a slow, laborious process. Frequently it took a whole day of exhausting effort to drag a single boulder to the top of the quarry, and sometimes when it was pushed over the edge it failed to break. Nothing could have been achieved without Boxer, whose strength seemed equal to that of all the rest of the animals put together. When the boulder began to slip and the animals cried out in despair at finding themselves dragged down the hill, it was always Boxer who strained himself against the rope and brought the boulder to a stop. To see him toiling up the slope inch by inch, his breath coming fast, the tips of his hoofs clawing at the ground, and his great sides **matted**^⑥ with sweat, filled everyone with admiration. Clover warned him sometimes to be careful not to overstrain himself, but Boxer would never listen to her. His two slogans, "I will work harder" and "Napoleon is always right," seemed to him a sufficient answer to all problems. He had made arrangements with the cockerel to call him three-quarters of an hour earlier in the mornings instead of half an hour. And in his spare moments, of which there were not many nowadays, he would go alone to the quarry, collect a load of broken stone, and drag it down to the site of the windmill unassisted.

The animals were not badly off throughout that summer, in spite of the hardness of their work. If they had no more food than they had had in Jones's day,

① utilise ['juːtilaiz] v. 利用
② boulder ['bəuldə] n. 圆石

③ topple ['tɔpl] v. 推倒

④ yoke [jəuk] v. 用轭连起来
⑤ superintendence
['sjuːpərin'tendəns] n. 监
督，指挥

⑥ mat [mæt] v. 使密集

石，但体积过大，无法派上用场。动物们现在用绳子拴住巨石，然后，奶牛、马、绵羊，一齐上阵，但凡能够抓住绳子的动物都上——有时候到了关键的时刻，连猪都得上阵了——速度极为缓慢，他们把巨石一点一点地拉到采石场的制高点。然后再把它往悬崖边推，巨石滚到下面便摔成碎块了。要运输摔碎的石块就比较简单了。马可以用车把石块拉走。绵羊可以拖单块石头，连白山羊穆里尔和毛驴本杰明都合着驾起了一辆老式轻便马车，尽着自己的一份力量。到了夏末，他们已经集中了足够多的石料，这时，建造工程在几头猪的指挥下开始了。

但是，工程进展缓慢，且颇费劳力。动物们往往要耗费一天时间，精疲力竭，才能把一块巨石拖到采石场的制高点。有时候，把巨石从悬崖处推下，却没有摔碎。拳击手力量巨大，似乎可以抵得上其他动物合起来的力量。若是没有他，那一定会一事无成。有时候，巨石开始向下滑动，动物们感觉自己也开始跟着向山坡下面掉，绝望地大声叫喊起来，拳击手总是会拼命地拉住绳子，让巨石止住。看着他铆足了力气把绳子一寸一寸往上拉，气喘吁吁，蹄子尖牢牢地扣住地面，硕大的身躯被汗水浸透，动物们一个个充满了敬佩之情。首蓿有时候会提醒他，要注意身体，不要劳累过度。但是，拳击手不会听她的劝告。对他而言，他的两句口头禅"我要更加卖力干活儿"和"拿破仑总是对的"似乎是对一切问题的最好回答。他已经同小公鸡约定好了，要小公鸡早晨提前三刻钟叫醒他，而不是提前半个小时。他在闲暇时间里，现在这样的闲暇不多了，会独自到采石场去，把碎石装满一车，拉到风车建造的场地上去，不需要任何动物的帮助。

整个夏天，动物们虽然工作繁重，但日子过得还不算很糟糕。即便他们的饲料并不比当初琼斯在的时

at least they did not have less. The advantage of only having to feed themselves, and not having to support five extravagant human beings as well, was so great that it would have taken a lot of failures to outweigh it. And in many ways the animal method of doing things was more efficient and saved labour. Such jobs as weeding, for instance, could be done with a thoroughness impossible to human beings. And again, since no animal now stole, it was unnecessary to fence off pasture from **arable**① land, which saved a lot of labour on the upkeep of hedges and gates. Nevertheless, as the summer wore on, various unforeseen shortages began to make themselves felt. There was need of **paraffin**② oil, **nails**③, string, dog biscuits, and iron for the horses' shoes, none of which could be produced on the farm. Later there would also be need for seeds and artificial manures, besides various tools and, finally, the machinery for the windmill. How these were to be procured, no one was able to imagine.

One Sunday morning, when the animals assembled to receive their orders, Napoleon announced that he had decided upon a new policy. From now onwards Animal Farm would engage in trade with the neighbouring farms: not, of course, for any commercial purpose, but simply in order to obtain certain materials which were urgently necessary. The needs of the windmill must override everything else, he said. He was therefore making arrangements to sell a stack of hay and part of the current year's wheat crop, and later on, if more money were needed, it would have to be made up by the sale of eggs, for which there was always a market in Willingdon. The hens, said Napoleon, should welcome this sacrifice as their own special contribution towards the building of the windmill.

Once again the animals were conscious of a vague uneasiness. Never to have any dealings with human beings, never to engage in trade, never to make use of money—had not these been among the earliest resolutions passed at that first triumphant Meeting after Jones was expelled? All the animals remembered passing such resolutions: or at least they thought that they remembered it. The four young pigs who had protested when Napoleon abolished the Meetings raised their voices **timidly**④, but they were promptly silenced by a tremendous

候丰富，但至少不至于比那个时候更匮乏。他们只需要喂饱自己，而无须再供养生活奢华的五口人。这种优越性显而易见，足以抵消掉大量工作中的失败。在很多方面，动物们做事的方法更加高效，更加省力。比如，清除杂草这一类的活儿，他们可以清除得一干二净，而换了人类那是绝不可能的。还有，由于动物当中没有了偷盗行为，牧场和耕地之间就没有必要用围栏隔开了，这样便节省了大量维护树篱和围栏的劳力。不过，随着夏季过去，出现了各种各样未曾料想到的短缺现象。农场上需要煤油、钉子、绳索、狗吃的饼干、马蹄铁，这些东西都不是农场上可以生产的。后来，除了不同种类的工具之外，还需要各种种子和化肥，还有建造风车所需的机械。这些东西如何才能得到满足，谁也想不出办法来。

有个星期天的上午，动物们聚集在一块儿接受劳动任务时，拿破仑宣布，他决定实施一项新政策。从今往后，动物农场将同附近的几座农场进行贸易活动：当然不是为了商业目的，而仅仅是为了获取一些急需的物品。满足建造风车的需要是当务之急，压倒一切，他是这样说的。因此，他做出了安排，准备卖掉一垛干草和当年收获的一部分小麦。随后，若是还需要资金，那就通过卖蛋来筹措，因为威灵登的市场一直都有销路。拿破仑说，母鸡应该勇于牺牲，以此作为自己对建造风车工程的一份特殊贡献。

动物们再次感到莫名地不安起来。决不同人类打交道，决不从事贸易活动，决不使用金钱，他们在驱逐琼斯后的第一聚会上，那些最早通过的决定中不是已经包含了这些条文吗？所有动物记得通过了这些决定：或者他们至少认为，他们记得这件事。当时拿破仑提出取消"会议"时，那四头小猪曾表示反对。他们此刻发出了怯生生的声音，但是，其声音立刻被狗的狂吠声掩盖掉了。然后，和平常一样，那些绵羊突然

① arable ['ærəbl] *a.* 适耕的
② paraffin ['pærəfin] *n.* 石蜡
③ nail [neil] *n.* 钉子

④ timidly ['timidli] *ad.* 羞怯地

growling from the dogs. Then, as usual, the sheep broke into "Four legs good, two legs bad!" and the momentary awkwardness was smoothed over. Finally Napoleon raised his trotter for silence and announced that he had already made all the arrangements. There would be no need for any of the animals to come in contact with human beings, which would clearly be most undesirable. He intended to take the whole burden upon his own shoulders. A Mr. Whymper, a **solicitor**① living in Willingdon, had agreed to act as intermediary between Animal Farm and the outside world, and would visit the farm every Monday morning to receive his instructions. Napoleon ended his speech with his usual cry of "Long live Animal Farm!" and after the singing of *Beasts of England* the animals were dismissed.

Afterwards Squealer made a round of the farm and set the animals' minds at rest. He assured them that the resolution against engaging in trade and using money had never been passed, or even suggested. It was pure imagination, probably **traceable**② in the beginning to lies circulated by Snowball. A few animals still felt faintly doubtful, but Squealer asked them shrewdly, "Are you certain that this is not something that you have dreamed, comrades? Have you any record of such a resolution? Is it written down anywhere?" And since it was certainly true that nothing of the kind existed in writing, the animals were satisfied that they had been mistaken.

Every Monday Mr. Whymper visited the farm as had been arranged. He was a sly-looking little man with side **whiskers**③, a solicitor in a very small way of business, but sharp enough to have realised earlier than anyone else that Animal Farm would need a broker and that the commissions would be worth having. The animals watched his coming and going with a kind of **dread**④, and avoided him as much as possible. Nevertheless, the sight of Napoleon, on all fours, delivering orders to Whymper, who stood on two legs, roused their pride and partly **reconciled**⑤ them to the new arrangement. Their relations with the human race were now not quite the same as they had been before. The human beings did not hate Animal Farm any less now that it was prospering; indeed, they hated it more

咩咩地念叨起"四条腿好，两条腿坏！"，短暂的尴尬局面化解掉了。最后，拿破仑抬起一只蹄子，示意肃静，并且宣布说，所有事项他都已经做出了安排。所有动物都无需同人类有任何接触，因为同人类接触是大家最不愿意做的事情。他打算把所有重担独自挑起来，有位名叫温佩尔的律师住在威灵登。他同意充任动物农场和外界的中间人。他每个星期一上午来动物农场接受吩咐。拿破仑还和平常一样，用高呼"动物农场万岁"的口号来结束自己的演讲。动物们唱过《英格兰的牲畜》后便四散开了。

过后，尖嗓子在农场兜了一圈，这才让动物们的心平静了下来。他向他们保证说，他们根本就没有通过禁止从事贸易活动和使用金钱的决定，甚至都没有提出过这方面的动议。这纯粹是凭着想象捏造出来的，或许可以追溯到开始时由雪球传播的谣言。少数一些动物仍然没有释然，心存疑虑，但尖嗓子显得很有策略，问他们："你们能够断定，这不是你们梦到过的一些事情吗，同志们？你们有这样一个决议的记录吗？决议是不是写在什么地方呢？"诸如此类的东西当然没有记录在案，动物们这才心服口服，是他们弄错了。

根据已经做出的安排，温佩尔先生每个星期一要拜访农场。他身材矮小，相貌诡异，长着络腮胡，是一位业务范围很狭窄的律师，但头脑精明，比谁都更早就看出了，动物农场需要一名经纪人，佣金可观。动物们目睹着他进进出出，心里怀着一种恐惧感，而且尽可能避开他。不过，他们看见四条腿走路的拿破仑对着两条腿走路的温佩尔先生发号施令时，心里洋溢着自豪感，从而对于这种新的安排也一定程度上释然了。同过去相比，他们现在与人类的关系不是一回事了。动物农场现在兴旺发达了，人类对它的仇视并没有因此减弱，事实上，比以往任何时候都更加强烈了。农场迟早要破产，尤其是，建造风车的工程会归于失败，

① solicitor [sə'lisitə] *n.* 律师

② traceable ['treisəbl] *a.* 可追踪的

③ whisker ['hwiskə] *n.* 腮须

④ dread [dred] *n.* 恐惧

⑤ reconcile ['rekənsail] *v.* 使顺从

than ever. Every human being held it as an article of faith that the farm would go **bankrupt**① sooner or later, and, above all, that the windmill would be a failure. They would meet in the public-houses and prove to one another by means of diagrams that the windmill was bound to fall down, or that if it did stand up, then that it would never work. And yet, against their will, they had developed a certain respect for the efficiency with which the animals were managing their own affairs. One symptom of this was that they had begun to call Animal Farm by its proper name and ceased to pretend that it was called the Manor Farm. They had also dropped their championship of Jones, who had given up hope of getting his farm back and gone to live in another part of the county. Except through Whymper, there was as yet no contact between Animal Farm and the outside world, but there were constant rumours that Napoleon was about to enter into a definite business agreement either with Mr. Pilkington of Foxwood or with Mr. Frederick of Pinchfield—but never, it was noticed, with both **simultaneously**②.

It was about this time that the pigs suddenly moved into the farmhouse and took up their residence there. Again the animals seemed to remember that a resolution against this had been passed in the early days, and again Squealer was able to convince them that this was not the case. It was absolutely necessary, he said, that the pigs, who were the brains of the farm, should have a quiet place to work in. It was also more suited to the dignity of the Leader (for of late he had taken to speaking of Napoleon under the title of "Leader") to live in a house than in a mere **sty**③. Nevertheless, some of the animals were disturbed when they heard that the pigs not only took their meals in the kitchen and used the drawing-room as a **recreation**④ room, but also slept in the beds. Boxer passed it off as usual with "Napoleon is always right!", but Clover, who thought she remembered a definite ruling against beds, went to the end of the barn and tried to puzzle out the Seven Commandments which were inscribed there. Finding herself unable to read more than individual letters, she fetched Muriel.

"Muriel," she said, "read me the Fourth Commandment. Does it not say something about never sleeping in a bed?"

① bankrupt ['bæŋkrʌpt] *a.* 破产的

这是每个人心里怀有的信念。人们聚集在酒馆里，通过图表的形式相互印证，风车注定要倒塌，或者，即便建造起来了，那也无法产生功效。不过，虽说并非出于意愿，但面对动物们有效地管理着他们自己的事务的情形，人们不由地产生了一种敬意。这方面的一个具体体现是，人们不再刻意称这座农场为"庄园农场"了，而开始使用"动物农场"这个名副其实的称谓。同时，他们也不再支持琼斯了，况且琼斯也已经放弃了夺回农场的一切希望，搬到本郡的另外一处地方居住了。除了通过温佩尔先生，动物农场迄今同外界还没有任何联系，但是，不断有传言，说拿破仑正准备同狐狸林农场的皮尔金顿先生或者窄地农场的弗里德里克先生签订一份实质性的业务协定——但是，大家注意到，不可能同时与两座农场有业务关系。

② simultaneously [,siməl'teiniəsli] *ad.* 同时地

　　大概也就是在这个时候，几头猪突然搬进了农场主住宅，并且在那儿居住下来了。动物们再次仿佛记得，早些时候他们通过了一个禁止这样做的决定，尖嗓子再次让他们相信，事实并非如此。他说，几头猪是农场上的脑力劳动者，需要有宁静的工作场所，所以，这样做绝对必要。再说，相对于住在猪圈里，住在房舍里更加符合领袖的尊贵地位（最近，他每次提到拿破仑时，都喜欢冠上"领袖"的头衔）。尽管如此，动物们可是听说了，那些猪不仅在厨房里用餐，把起居室用作娱乐室，而且还睡在床上。这时候，他们中有

③ sty [stai] *n.* 猪圈
④ recreation [,rekri'eiʃən] *n.* 娱乐

一些感到心烦意乱。拳击手还是一如既往，用"拿破仑总是对的！"这句话圆了过去。但是，苜蓿感觉自己记得，有过明确的规定，不允许睡床。她走到了大谷仓尽头的外墙边，猜谜似的想要琢磨清楚书写在那儿的"七戒"条文。她发现自己只能认出一些字母，便去找来了穆里尔。

　　"穆里尔，"她说，"把'第四戒'念给我听吧。那上面不是说到了决不能睡在床上吗？"

With some difficulty Muriel spelt it out.

"It says, 'No animal shall sleep in a bed *with sheets*,'" she announced finally.

Curiously enough, Clover had not remembered that the Fourth Command-ment mentioned sheets; but as it was there on the wall, it must have done so. And Squealer, who happened to be passing at this moment, attended by two or three dogs, was able to put the whole matter in its proper perspective.

"You have heard then, comrades," he said, "that we pigs now sleep in the beds of the farmhouse? And why not? You did not suppose, surely, that there was ever a ruling against beds? A bed merely means a place to sleep in. A pile of straw in a stall is a bed, properly regarded. The rule was against sheets, which are a human invention. We have removed the sheets from the farmhouse beds, and sleep between blankets. And very comfortable beds they are too! But not more comfortable than we need, I can tell you, comrades, with all the brainwork we have to do nowadays. You would not rob us of our **repose**①, would you, comrades? You would not have us too tired to carry out our duties? Surely none of you wishes to see Jones back?"

The animals reassured him on this point immediately, and no more was said about the pigs sleeping in the farmhouse beds. And when, some days afterwards, it was announced that from now on the pigs would get up an hour later in the mornings than the other animals, no complaint was made about that either.

By the autumn the animals were tired but happy. They had had a hard year, and after the sale of part of the hay and corn, the stores of food for the winter were none too plentiful, but the windmill **compensated**② for everything. It was almost half built now. After the harvest there was a stretch of clear dry weather, and the animals toiled harder than ever, thinking it well worthwhile to **plod**③

穆里尔费了一些劲儿才拼读了出来。

"上面说的是，'任何动物都不睡在**有被单**的床上'。"她最后说。

苜蓿觉得很不可思议，明明记得"第四戒"没有提到被单，但字已经写在墙壁上，那就一定是这么回事。尖嗓子此刻正好路过，有两三条狗陪同着。他能够从合适的角度把问题说清楚。

"这么说来，同志们，"他说，"你们已经听说我们猪要睡在农场主住宅的床上了？为什么不呢？毫无疑问，你们并不会认为，什么时候有过一条关于禁止使用床的条文吧？一张床，简单说起来就是一个睡觉的地方而已。准确说起来，厩棚里面的一堆干草是一张床。戒律禁止的床单，那是人类发明的东西。我们已经从住宅里的床上把床单掀掉了，盖的是毯子。床上有毯子盖着也舒适啊！但是，舒适的程度离我们所需要的还有差距呢，我可以告诉你们，同志们啊，因为我们现如今必须从事脑力劳动。你们不会不让我们好好休息吧，同志们？你们不会要把我们给弄得精疲力竭以至不能履行职责吧？毫无疑问，你们谁都不愿意看到琼斯再回来，对吧？"

关于这一点，动物们的态度立刻便让他放心了。有关猪睡在住宅床上的事情，谁也没有再说什么。不过，一些日子过后，农场上宣布，从今往后，猪比其他动物晚起床一个小时。动物们知道了这件事情后，也同样没有任何抱怨。

秋天来了，动物们很劳累，但很快乐。他们艰苦劳作了一年，卖掉了一部分干草和谷物之后，仓库里用于过冬的饲料已经不是很丰富了，但是，风车足以弥补这一切。工程现在差不多完成了一半了。收割季节过后，天气有很长一段时间干燥晴朗，动物们干活儿比先前更加卖力了。他们寻思着，他们整天来来回回，搬运着石料，只要这样做可以让墙壁再增高一英尺，那他们的劳

① repose [ri'pəuz] *n.* 休息

② compensate ['kɔmpenseit] *v.* 抵消

③ plod [plɔd] *v.* 沉闷地苦干

to and fro all day with blocks of stone if by doing so they could raise the walls another foot. Boxer would even come out at nights and work for an hour or two on his own by the light of the harvest moon. In their spare moments the animals would walk round and round the half-finished mill, admiring the strength and **perpendicularity**① of its walls and marvelling that they should ever have been able to build anything so **imposing**②. Only old Benjamin refused to grow enthusiastic about the windmill, though, as usual, he would utter nothing beyond the cryptic remark that donkeys live a long time.

November came, with raging south-west winds. Building had to stop because it was now too wet to mix the cement. Finally there came a night when the **gale**③ was so violent that the farm buildings rocked on their foundations and several **tiles**④ were blown off the roof of the barn. The hens woke up **squawking**⑤ with terror because they had all dreamed simultaneously of hearing a gun go off in the distance. In the morning the animals came out of their stalls to find that the flagstaff had been blown down and an elm tree at the foot of the orchard had been **plucked**⑥ up like a **radish**⑦. They had just noticed this when a cry of despair broke from every animal's throat. A terrible sight had met their eyes. The windmill was in ruins.

With one accord they dashed down to the spot. Napoleon, who seldom moved out of a walk, raced ahead of them all. Yes, there it lay, the fruit of all their struggles, levelled to its foundations, the stones they had broken and carried so laboriously scattered all around. Unable at first to speak, they stood gazing mournfully at the litter of fallen stone. Napoleon paced to and fro in silence, occasionally snuffing at the ground. His tail had grown rigid and twitched sharply from side to side, a sign in him of intense mental activity.

Suddenly he halted as though his mind were made up.

"Comrades," he said quietly, "do you know who is responsible for this? Do you know the enemy who has come in the night and overthrown our windmill?

累就是值得的。拳击手甚至会趁着获月[1]期间的月色夜间外出，独自干上一两个小时的活儿。空余时间里，动物们会绕着工期完成了一半的风车现场一圈一圈地转，怀着敬佩之情欣赏着坚固垂直的墙壁，内心里不禁赞叹了起来，他们竟然能够建造出如此气势恢宏的工程。只有年迈的本杰明没有对风车工程表现出热情，不过，他还和平常一样，嘴里除了说驴子寿命很长那句神秘莫测的话之外，三缄其口。

十一月了，西南风呼啸着。动物们不得不中止施工，因为这时候阴雨连绵，无法拌水泥。最后，一天夜里，狂风大作，农场上的窝棚整体摇摇晃晃，大谷仓顶上有一些瓦片都被风刮走了。母鸡们醒来后，惊恐不已，咯咯乱叫，因为她们同时在睡梦中听见了远处传来枪响声。翌日早晨，动物从自己的窝棚里出来，发现旗杆吹倒了，果园下端的一棵榆树像个萝卜似的被连根拔起。他们刚刚注意到了这一点，突然，每一只动物都从喉咙挤出绝望的喊声。眼前出现恐怖的一幕：风车建设工地成了一片废墟。

动物们同时间冲向现场。拿破仑平时极少移步室外，此时冲在他们的最前头。是啊，建筑倒塌了，所有动物共同的成果，全都夷为平地了。他们历尽艰辛，碎开并费力搬运来的石头四处散落着。他们刚一开始时话都说不出来，就那么站着，神情悲伤地注视着散落一地的碎石块。拿破仑默不作声，来回踱着步，时不时地对着地面嗅一嗅。他的尾巴变得很僵硬了，猛烈地左右摆动，这是他内心紧张的表现。

他突然停住了脚步，好像已经做出了什么决定。

"同志们，"他说，语气很平静，"你们知道谁应该对这个结果负责吗？你们知道夜间进入农场推翻我们这座风车建筑的敌人是谁吗？雪球啊！"他突然提高嗓门，

① perpendicularity ['pəːpen.dikju'læriti] *n.* 垂直
② imposing [im'pəuziŋ] *a.* 壮观的

③ gale [geil] *n.* 狂风
④ tile [tail] *n.* 瓦片
⑤ squawk [skwɔːk] *v.* 发出响耳粗的叫声

⑥ pluck [plʌk] *v.* 拉
⑦ radish ['rædiʃ] *n.* 萝卜

---

1 获月（harvest moon）指 9 月 22 日或 23 日秋分后两个星期内的第一次满月。

Snowball!" he suddenly roared in a voice of thunder. "Snowball has done this thing! In sheer **malignity**①, thinking to set back our plans and **avenge**② himself for his **ignominious**③ expulsion, this traitor has crept here under cover of night and destroyed our work of nearly a year. Comrades, here and now I pronounce the death sentence upon Snowball. 'Animal Hero, Second Class,' and half a bushel of apples to any animal who brings him to justice. A full bushel to anyone who captures him alive!"

The animals were shocked beyond measure to learn that even Snowball could be guilty of such an action. There was a cry of **indignation**④, and everyone began thinking out ways of catching Snowball if he should ever come back. Almost immediately the footprints of a pig were discovered in the grass at a little distance from the knoll. They could only be traced for a few yards, but appeared to lead to a hole in the hedge. Napoleon snuffed deeply at them and pronounced them to be Snowball's. He gave it as his opinion that Snowball had probably come from the direction of Foxwood Farm.

"No more delays, comrades!" cried Napoleon when the footprints had been examined. "There is work to be done. This very morning we begin rebuilding the windmill, and we will build all through the winter, rain or shine. We will teach this miserable traitor that he cannot undo our work so easily. Remember, comrades, there must be no **alteration**⑤ in our plans: they shall be carried out to the day. Forward, comrades! Long live the windmill! Long live Animal Farm!"

① malignity [mə'ligniti] *n.* 狠毒

② avenge [ə'vendʒ] *v.* 为……报复

③ ignominious [.ignəu'miniəs] *a.* 耻辱的

如惊雷一般，"雪球制造了这一切！那个十恶不赦的叛徒用心险恶，处心积虑地要阻止我们实现计划，要为自己遭受驱逐的耻辱报仇雪恨。他趁着夜色悄悄潜入农场，毁掉了我们几乎花费了一年功夫的工程。同志们，我现在宣布，对雪球判处死刑。任何将他就地正法的动物可以授予'二级动物英雄'勋章，还可以奖励半个蒲式耳苹果。如若有动物生擒了雪球，那就奖励一个蒲式耳的苹果！"

④ indignation [.indig'neiʃən] *n.* 愤怒

动物们得知连雪球都会犯下如此罪行，感到无比震惊，顿时响起了一片愤怒的叫声。每只动物都在考虑，一旦雪球回来了，该如何逮住他。几乎就在片刻之后，有动物在山丘不远处的草丛中发现了猪蹄印子。猪蹄印子只持续了几码远的距离，但是似乎延伸到树篱边的一个缺口处了。拿破仑深深地嗅了嗅那些猪蹄印子，宣称是雪球的。他表达了自己的看法，雪球很有可能是从狐狸林农场那个方向过来的。

⑤ alteration [.ɔ:ltə'reiʃən] *n.* 改变

"不能再耽搁了，同志们！"拿破仑仔细查看过了猪蹄印子后说，"我们还有活儿要干呢。从今天上午开始，我们着手重新建造风车，整个冬季，无论天晴下雨，我们都要坚持建造。我们要让那位卑鄙的叛徒看看，他想要破坏我们的工程，可没有那么容易。请记住，同志们，我们的计划不可能有任何改变，而且一定要如期完成。前进吧，同志们！风车万岁！动物农场万岁！"

Chapter VII

It was a bitter winter. The stormy weather was followed by **sleet**① and snow, and then by a hard frost which did not break till well into February. The animals carried on as best they could with the rebuilding of the windmill, well knowing that the outside world was watching them and that the envious human beings would **rejoice**② and triumph if the mill were not finished on time.

Out of **spite**③, the human beings pretended not to believe that it was Snowball who had destroyed the windmill: they said that it had fallen down because the walls were too thin. The animals knew that this was not the case. Still, it had been decided to build the walls three feet thick this time instead of eighteen inches as before, which meant collecting much larger quantities of stone. For a long time the quarry was full of snowdrifts and nothing could be done. Some progress was made in the dry frosty weather that followed, but it was cruel work, and the animals could not feel so hopeful about it as they had felt before. They were always cold, and usually hungry as well. Only Boxer and Clover never lost heart. Squealer made excellent speeches on the joy of service and the dignity of labour, but the other animals found more inspiration in Boxer's strength and his never-failing cry of "I will work harder!"

In January food fell short. The corn ration was **drastically**④ reduced, and it was announced that an extra potato ration would be issued to make up for it.

第七章

① sleet [sli:t] *n.* 雨雹

② rejoice [ri'dʒɔis] *v.* 欣喜
③ spite [spait] *n.* 怨恨

④ drastically ['dræstikəli] *ad.* 激烈地

这是个严寒的冬季。暴风雨天气过后，又是冻雨又是大雪的，随后是天寒地冻，一直持续到了二月。动物们竭尽全力，坚持奋战在重建风车的工地上，心里很清楚，外界一直在注视着他们，倘若风车不能如期竣工，充满了嫉妒心的人类一定会高兴不已。

出于仇恨的心理，人类假装不相信是雪球摧毁了风车：他们说，风车之所以倒塌，是因为墙体太薄了。动物们知道，情况并非如此。尽管如此，他们还是决定，墙壁的厚度由先前的十八英寸增加到三英尺，这就意味着要收集更多石料。很长一段时间里，采石场布满了积雪，根本无法开工。等到随后出现了干冷天气，工程才稍有进展，但那是十分艰辛的活儿。关于风车工程，动物们不可能像先前那样充满希望了。他们一直忍受着寒冷和饥饿。只有拳击手和首蓿从未心灰意冷过。尖嗓子巧舌如簧，大谈服务的快乐，劳动的尊严。但是，其他动物所受到的鼓舞，更多的还是来自拳击手旺盛的精力和他那句念念不忘的"我要更加卖力干活儿"的话。

到了一月，饲料出现短缺。谷物饲料的配额急剧缩减。农场宣布，要施行额外的土豆配额，以弥补不足。随后，动物们发现，由于覆盖物不够厚实，收进来后堆

Then it was discovered that the greater part of the potato crop had been frosted in the clamps, which had not been covered thickly enough. The potatoes had become soft and discoloured, and only a few were **edible**①. For days at a time the animals had nothing to eat but **chaff**② and mangels. Starvation seemed to stare them in the face.

It was vitally necessary to conceal this fact from the outside world. **Emboldened**③ by the collapse of the windmill, the human beings were inventing fresh lies about Animal Farm. Once again it was being put about that all the animals were dying of famine and disease, and that they were continually fighting among themselves and had resorted to cannibalism and **infanticide**④. Napoleon was well aware of the bad results that might follow if the real facts of the food situation were known, and he decided to make use of Mr. Whymper to spread a contrary impression. **Hitherto**⑤ the animals had had little or no contact with Whymper on his weekly visits: now, however, a few selected animals, mostly sheep, were instructed to remark casually in his hearing that rations had been increased. In addition, Napoleon ordered the almost empty bins in the store-shed to be filled nearly to the brim with sand, which was then covered up with what remained of the grain and meal. On some suitable pretext Whymper was led through the store-shed and allowed to catch a glimpse of the bins. He was deceived, and continued to report to the outside world that there was no food shortage on Animal Farm.

Nevertheless, towards the end of January it became obvious that it would be necessary to procure some more grain from somewhere. In these days Napoleon rarely appeared in public, but spent all his time in the farmhouse, which was guarded at each door by fierce-looking dogs. When he did emerge, it was in a ceremonial manner, with an **escort**⑥ of six dogs who closely surrounded him and growled if anyone came too near. Frequently he did not even appear on Sunday mornings, but issued his orders through one of the other pigs, usually Squealer.

One Sunday morning Squealer announced that the hens, who had just come in to lay again, must surrender their eggs. Napoleon had accepted, through

积在一块儿的土豆受了冻，柔软变色了，只有极少部分可以食用。有时候一连几天，动物们只能吃谷糠和甜菜。看起来，他们面临着饥荒了。

① edible ['edibl] *a.* 可食（用）的
② chaff [tʃɑ:f] *n.* 谷壳

③ embolden [im'bəuldən] *v.* 给……壮胆

④ infanticide [in'fæntisaid] *n.* 杀害婴儿
⑤ hitherto [.hiðə'tu:] *ad.* 迄今

⑥ escort ['eskɔ:t] *n.* 陪同

一定要对外界隐瞒这个事实，这一点至关重要。风车倒塌后，人类的腰杆子挺直了。他们正编造着关于动物农场的新谣言。到处又在风传着，说所有动物忍饥挨饿，疾病缠身，挣扎在死亡线上。动物内部争斗不断，而且故态复萌，互相残食，宰杀幼崽。拿破仑心知肚明，外界若是知晓了他们饲料供应的真实状况，将会产生多么严重的后果。他决定启用温佩尔先生，要让他传播一些相反的印象。迄今为止，温佩尔先生每个星期光顾农场时，动物们极少同他接触。不过，现在，拿破仑精挑细选了极少数动物，主要是绵羊，吩咐他们议论饲料增加的事情，语气要显得若无其事，让温佩尔先生听到。此外，拿破仑还责令动物们把饲料棚内那些差不多空了的饲料槽装上沙子，装到快要满了，再把仅存的一点点谷物饲料覆盖在面上。找到合适的借口，把温佩尔先生领进饲料棚，让他看一看那些饲料槽。受了蒙骗之后，他继续对外界报告说，动物农场不存在饲料短缺的问题。

尽管如此，到了一月底时，情况已经很明显了，必须要想方设法从哪儿再弄到一些饲料。那些日子里，拿破仑极少在公众面前抛头露面，而是整天待在农场主住宅里。住宅里的每一道门都由面目狰狞的狗把守着。拿破仑即便在外面亮相，那也是八面威风，犹如盛典，六条狗如影随形，相伴左右。若是有哪只动物靠得太近，狗便会狂吠起来。即便是在星期天，拿破仑都常常不露面，而是通过其他猪宣布他的指令，通常是通过尖嗓子。

有个星期天上午，尖嗓子宣布，所有开始下蛋的母鸡都必须把蛋交出来。通过温佩尔先生，拿破仑已经签

Whymper, a contract for four hundred eggs a week. The price of these would pay for enough grain and meal to keep the farm going till summer came on and conditions were easier.

When the hens heard this, they raised a terrible outcry. They had been warned earlier that this sacrifice might be necessary, but had not believed that it would really happen. They were just getting their clutches ready for the spring sitting, and they protested that to take the eggs away now was murder. For the first time since the expulsion of Jones, there was something **resembling**[1] a rebellion. Led by three young Black Minorca **pullets**[2], the hens made a determined effort to **thwart**[3] Napoleon's wishes. Their method was to fly up to the rafters and there lay their eggs, which smashed to pieces on the floor. Napoleon acted swiftly and **ruthlessly**[4]. He ordered the hens' rations to be stopped, and **decreed**[5] that any animal giving so much as a grain of corn to a hen should be punished by death. The dogs saw to it that these orders were carried out. For five days the hens held out, then they **capitulated**[6] and went back to their nesting boxes. Nine hens had died in the meantime. Their bodies were buried in the orchard, and it was given out that they had died of **coccidiosis**[7]. Whymper heard nothing of this affair, and the eggs were duly delivered, a grocer's **van**[8] driving up to the farm once a week to take them away.

All this while no more had been seen of Snowball. He was rumoured to be hiding on one of the neighbouring farms, either Foxwood or Pinchfield. Napoleon was by this time on slightly better terms with the other farmers than before. It happened that there was in the yard a pile of **timber**[9] which had been stacked there ten years earlier when a **beech**[10] **spinney**[11] was cleared. It was well seasoned, and Whymper had advised Napoleon to sell it; both Mr. Pilkington and Mr. Frederick were anxious to buy it. Napoleon was hesitating between the two, unable to make up his mind. It was noticed that whenever he seemed on the point of coming to an agreement with Frederick, Snowball was declared to be in hiding at Foxwood, while, when he inclined toward Pilkington, Snowball was said to be at Pinchfield.

订了一份每个星期提供四百枚鸡蛋的合同。鸡蛋出售后所得收入可购买到足够多的谷物和饲料，让农场维持到夏天情况好转了。

母鸡听到这个决定后，大惊失色，咯咯大叫了起来。她们早些时候便得到了提醒，说有可能需要她们做出这样的牺牲，但她们不相信事情果然会发生。她们其实已经积攒齐了蛋，准备春季坐窝来着。她们抗议着说，要把她们下的蛋拿走，这无异于谋杀。自从琼斯被驱逐之后，头一次出现了这样的反抗集会。由三只米诺卡小黑鸡[1]领头，母鸡们决定搏一把，挫败拿破仑的计划。她们使用的方法是，飞到椽子上去下蛋，蛋掉落到地上就摔碎了。拿破仑迅速采取行动，残忍无情。他责令停止给母鸡发放饲料。而且还下令，若是有动物给母鸡哪怕是一粒谷物，都要被处以死刑。那些狗负责落实这两道命令。母鸡们坚持了五天，最后还是就范了，返回到了她们的窝里。这期间，死了六只母鸡。她们的遗体被掩埋在果园中。对外的说法是，她们死于球虫病。温佩尔对这件事情毫不知情，因为农场按时提供了鸡蛋。有辆食物专用篷车每个星期开进一次农场来把鸡蛋运走。

整个这段时间里，谁也没有看见过雪球。有传言说，他藏匿在附近的一座农场，或在狐狸林，或在窄地。相比从前，拿破仑这段时间里同其他农场的关系略有改善。院落里正好有一堆木材。十年前，农场清理一片山毛榉树林时，木材就堆在那儿了。木材已经完全风干，温佩尔建议拿破仑把木材卖了。皮尔金顿和弗里德里克两个人都迫切想要购买。拿破仑举棋不定，不知道该卖给他们哪一位。大家注意到，每当他似乎快要同弗里德里克达成协议时，就会有动物报告说，雪球藏匿在狐狸林农场。而当他倾向于同皮尔金顿签约时，就会有动物来报告说，雪球藏匿在窄地农场。

1　米诺卡鸡（Minorca）是一种西班牙蛋用鸡，羽毛有黑、白、黄等颜色。

① resemble [ri'zembl] v. 类似

② pullet ['pulit] n. 小母鸡

③ thwart [θwɔ:t] v. 反对；阻挠

④ ruthlessly ['ru:θlisli] ad. 残忍地

⑤ decree [di'kri:] v. 发布（命令）

⑥ capitulate [kə'pitjuleit] v. 停止抵抗

⑦ coccidiosis [kɔk,sidi'əusis] n. 球虫病

⑧ van [væn] n. 大篷货车

⑨ timber ['timbə] n. 木材
⑩ beech ['bi:tʃ] n. 山毛榉
⑪ spinney ['spini] n. 矮林

Suddenly, early in the spring, an alarming thing was discovered. Snowball was secretly frequenting the farm by night! The animals were so disturbed that they could hardly sleep in their stalls. Every night, it was said, he came creeping in under cover of darkness and performed all kinds of mischief. He stole the corn, he upset the milk-pails, he broke the eggs, he trampled the seedbeds, he **gnawed**① the **bark**② off the fruit trees. Whenever anything went wrong it became usual to attribute it to Snowball. If a window was broken or a drain was blocked up, someone was certain to say that Snowball had come in the night and done it, and when the key of the store-shed was lost, the whole farm was convinced that Snowball had thrown it down the well. Curiously enough, they went on believing this even after the mislaid key was found under a **sack**③ of meal. The cows declared unanimously that Snowball crept into their stalls and milked them in their sleep. The rats, which had been troublesome that winter, were also said to be in league with Snowball.

Napoleon decreed that there should be a full investigation into Snowball's activities. With his dogs in attendance he set out and made a careful tour of inspection of the farm buildings, the other animals following at a respectful distance. At every few steps Napoleon stopped and snuffed the ground for traces of Snowball's footsteps, which, he said, he could detect by the smell. He snuffed in every corner, in the barn, in the cow-shed, in the henhouses, in the vegetable garden, and found traces of Snowball almost everywhere. He would put his **snout**④ to the ground, give several deep sniffs, and exclaim in a terrible voice, "Snowball! He has been here! I can smell him distinctly!" and at the word "Snowball" all the dogs let out blood-curdling growls and showed their side teeth.

The animals were thoroughly frightened. It seemed to them as though Snowball were some kind of invisible influence, **pervading**⑤ the air about them and menacing them with all kinds of dangers. In the evening Squealer called them together, and with an alarmed expression on his face told them that he had some serious news to report.

开春时节，农场上突然发生了一件令人惊诧的事情。雪球夜间秘密潜入了农场！动物们惊恐不安起来，几乎无法在自己的窝棚睡踏实觉。据说，雪球每天夜里都会趁着夜色潜入农场，进行各种各样的破坏捣乱活动：盗窃谷物、打翻奶桶、捣碎鸡蛋、踩踏苗圃、啃咬果树皮。但凡出了什么乱子，动物们都会习惯地把它归咎到雪球头上。倘若某块窗户玻璃打破了，某处下水道堵塞了，某只动物肯定会说，雪球夜间来过了，是他干的。若是饲料棚的钥匙丢了，整座农场的动物都相信，是雪球把钥匙扔进井里面了。很不可思议的是，即便后来发现，钥匙是被不知哪位动物错放在了饲料袋下面，动物们还是相信上面的说法。奶牛们口径一致地声称，雪球夜间潜入到她们的窝棚里，趁着她们熟睡之际挤走了奶。耗子们冬天里够捣乱的，据说他们同雪球勾结在一块儿了。

拿破仑下达了命令，关于雪球的种种行径，必须来一次彻底调查。他开始对农场的窝棚来一次仔细认真的查看，那些狗陪伴在他左右，其他动物充满着敬仰之情，远远地跟在后面。拿破仑每走上几步便会驻足不前，嗅一嗅地面，寻找雪球蹄子印的蛛丝马迹，因为他说了，他可以嗅出雪球的蹄子印。他嗅过了每一个角落，包括大谷仓、奶牛棚、母鸡舍、菜园。他几乎在每一处地方都发现了雪球的踪迹。他会把口鼻凑近地面，深深地吸气，然后情绪激动地发出恐怖的声音："雪球！他到过这儿呢！我能够清晰地嗅出他的气味来！"那些狗听到"雪球"这两个字时，全都张开了血盆大口，露出獠牙，狂吠起来。

动物们给彻底地吓坏了。他们似乎觉得，雪球是某种看不见摸不着的影响力量，弥散在他们的周围，威胁着他们，让他们感受到所有危险。傍晚时分，尖嗓子把动物们召集到一块儿，脸上流露出惊恐不安的表情，告诉动物们，他要公布一条重要消息。

① gnaw [nɔ:] v. 咬断，咬坏
② bark [bɑ:k] n. 树皮

③ sack [sæk] n. 麻袋

④ snout [snaut] n.（动物的）口鼻部

⑤ pervade [pə'veid] v. 弥漫

"Comrades!" cried Squealer, making little nervous skips, "a most terrible thing has been discovered. Snowball has sold himself to Frederick of Pinchfield Farm, who is even now plotting to attack us and take our farm away from us! Snowball is to act as his guide when the attack begins. But there is worse than that. We had thought that Snowball's rebellion was caused simply by his vanity and ambition. But we were wrong, comrades. Do you know what the real reason was? Snowball was in league with Jones from the very start! He was Jones's secret agent all the time. It has all been proved by documents which he left behind him and which we have only just discovered. To my mind this explains a great deal, comrades. Did we not see for ourselves how he attempted fortunately without success to get us defeated and destroyed at the Battle of the Cowshed?"

The animals were **stupefied**①. This was a wickedness far outdoing Snowball's destruction of the windmill. But it was some minutes before they could fully take it in. They all remembered, or thought they remembered, how they had seen Snowball charging ahead of them at the Battle of the Cowshed, how he had **rallied**② and encouraged them at every turn, and how he had not paused for an instant even when the pellets from Jones's gun had wounded his back. At first it was a little difficult to see how this fitted in with his being on Jones's side. Even Boxer, who seldom asked questions, was puzzled. He lay down, **tucked**③ his fore hoofs beneath him, shut his eyes, and with a hard effort managed to **formulate**④ his thoughts.

"I do not believe that," he said. "Snowball fought bravely at the Battle of the Cowshed. I saw him myself. Did we not give him 'Animal Hero, first Class,' immediately afterwards?"

"That was our mistake, comrade. For we know now it is all written down in the secret documents that we have found that in reality he was trying to **lure**⑤ us to our doom."

"But he was wounded," said Boxer. "We all saw him running with blood."

"同志们！"尖嗓子大声说，身子稍稍紧张地蹦了蹦，"我们已经发现了一件十分可怕的事情。雪球已经把自己出卖给窄地农场的弗里德里克了。此人正蠢蠢欲动，设计对我们发起进攻，把农场从我们手上抢夺过去！进攻行动一旦开始，雪球拟担任向导。但是，还有比这更加糟糕的情况。我们先前认为，雪球之所以有了反叛之心，纯粹是虚荣和野心作祟。但是，我们想错了，同志们啊，你们知道真实原因是什么吗？雪球从一开始便与琼斯狼狈为奸！长期以来，他一直充当琼斯的密探。他留下了一些文件，我们刚刚发现了那些文件。这一切从文件中得到了证明。我觉得这已经很说明问题啦，同志们。'牛棚之战'爆发时，幸运的是，他的企图没有得逞，没有让我们全军覆没。这一点我们不是都已经亲眼见识过了吗？"

动物们目瞪口呆。这一招可比雪球摧毁风车要邪恶得多啊。但是，过了好几分钟，他们才完全领悟过来。他们全都记得，或者认为自己记得，"牛棚之战"中，他们看到雪球如何一马当先，冲锋在前。他如何在每一个关键时刻鼓舞大家的士气，振作起大家的精神。即便在琼斯举枪射击，子弹伤着他的背部时，他也片刻都没有停止战斗。起初，他们一时间难以理解，雪球怎么会站在琼斯一边。连极少提出疑问的拳击手都感到迷惑不解了。他躺了下来，两个前蹄曲在身子的下面，闭上眼睛，费心劳神地想要理清自己的思路。

"我不相信这个说法，"他说，"'牛棚之战'中，雪球英勇无畏，我是亲眼见识过的。我们事后不是立刻授予他'一级动物英雄'勋章了吗？"

"那是我们的失误啊，同志。我们现在已经知道了，他实际上想要让我们走向灭亡，这一切都在那些秘密文件中记载着呢。"

"但他负了伤啊，"拳击手说，"我们都看见他流着血还在奔跑来着。"

① stupefy ['stju:pifai] v. 使茫然

② rally ['ræli] v. 重整（溃军等）

③ tuck [tʌk] v. 把（两腿）蜷曲在胸前
④ formulate ['fɔ:mjuleit] v. 构想出

⑤ lure [ljuə] n. 引诱

"That was part of the arrangement!" cried Squealer. "Jones's shot only **grazed**① him. I could show you this in his own writing, if you were able to read it. The plot was for Snowball, at the critical moment, to give the signal for flight and leave the field to the enemy. And he very nearly succeeded, I will even say, comrades, he would have succeeded if it had not been for our heroic Leader, Comrade Napoleon. Do you not remember how, just at the moment when Jones and his men had got inside the yard, Snowball suddenly turned and fled, and many animals followed him? And do you not remember, too, that it was just at that moment, when panic was spreading and all seemed lost, that Comrade Napoleon sprang forward with a cry of 'Death to Humanity!' and sank his teeth in Jones's leg? Surely you remember that, comrades?" exclaimed Squealer, frisking from side to side.

Now when Squealer described the scene so graphically, it seemed to the animals that they did remember it. At any rate, they remembered that at the critical moment of the battle Snowball had turned to flee. But Boxer was still a little uneasy.

"I do not believe that Snowball was a traitor at the beginning," he said finally. "What he has done since is different. But I believe that at the Battle of the Cowshed he was a good comrade."

"Our Leader, Comrade Napoleon," announced Squealer, speaking very slowly and firmly, "has stated **categorically**②, comrade, that Snowball was Jones's agent from the very beginning, yes, and from long before the Rebellion was ever thought of."

"Ah, that is different!" said Boxer. "If Comrade Napoleon says it, it must be right."

"That is the true spirit, comrade!" cried Squealer, but it was noticed he cast a very ugly look at Boxer with his little twinkling eyes. He turned to go, then paused and added impressively: "I warn every animal on this farm to keep his eyes very wide open. For we have reason to think that some of Snowball's secret agents are **lurking**③ among us at this moment!"

① graze [greiz] *v.* 擦伤

"那是他事先安排好了的！"尖嗓子大声说，"琼斯开的那一枪仅仅擦伤了他的一点皮毛。你若是能够看懂，我可以把他自己写的东西给你看。他们事先密谋好了，关键时刻，雪球发出撤离的信号，把阵地留给敌人。他几乎就得逞了。我甚至可以说，同志们，若不是有了我们英勇的领袖拿破仑同志，他就得逞了。就在琼斯和他的人进入院落的当儿，雪球突然转身逃跑，很多动物都跟随着他。这一点你们难道都不记得了吗？就在那个时刻，恐怖的气氛蔓延着，一切似乎都完了，拿破仑同志挺身而出，大喊着'消灭人类！'的口号，同时咬住琼斯的一条腿，这一点你们难道也不记得了吗？你们毫无疑问记得吧，同志们？"尖嗓子激动地说，身子左蹦右跳着。

尖嗓子活灵活现地描述着当时的场景，动物们似乎觉得，他们确实记起来了。不管怎么说，他们记得，战斗的关键时刻，雪球转身逃窜了。但是，拳击手心里还是有点不踏实。

"我并不相信雪球从一开始就是叛徒，"他最后说，"他后来的行为另当别论。但是，我相信，'牛棚之战'中，他是个好同志。"

② categorically [ˌkæti'gɔːrikli] *ad.* 直截了当地

"我们的领袖拿破仑同志，"尖嗓子宣布说，话说得很慢，语气坚定，"十分明确地指出了，雪球从一开始就是琼斯的密探，是啊，早在大家还没有想到要举行反抗运动之前很久就是了。"

"啊，那就另当别论了！"拳击手说，"如果拿破仑同志都这么说了，那就一定是对的。"

"这才是正确的认识啊，同志！"尖嗓子大声说，但是，大家都注意到，他那双闪闪发亮的小眼睛看拳击手时，流露出可怕的目光。他转身离开，紧接着停住了脚步，语气严厉地补充说，"我要警告本农场的每一只动物，睁开他的眼睛注意看着。因为我有理由认为，此时此刻，雪球的密探正潜藏在我们中间呢！"

③ lurk [ləːk] *v.* 潜伏

Four days later, in the late afternoon, Napoleon ordered all the animals to assemble in the yard. When they were all gathered together, Napoleon emerged from the farmhouse, wearing both his medals (for he had recently awarded himself "Animal Hero, First Class," and "Animal Hero, Second Class"), with his nine huge dogs frisking round him and uttering growls that sent shivers down all the animals' **spines**①. They all **cowered**② silently in their places, seeming to know in advance that some terrible thing was about to happen.

Napoleon stood sternly surveying his audience; then he uttered a high-pitched whimper. Immediately the dogs bounded forward, seized four of the pigs by the ear and dragged them, squealing with pain and terror, to Napoleon's feet. The pigs' ears were bleeding, the dogs had tasted blood, and for a few moments they appeared to go quite mad. To the amazement of everybody, three of them flung themselves upon Boxer. Boxer saw them coming and put out his great hoof, caught a dog in mid-air, and pinned him to the ground. The dog **shrieked**③ for mercy and the other two fled with their tails between their legs. Boxer looked at Napoleon to know whether he should crush the dog to death or let it go. Napoleon appeared to change **countenance**④, and sharply ordered Boxer to let the dog go, whereat Boxer lifted his hoof, and the dog **slunk**⑤ away, bruised and howling.

Presently the **tumult**⑥ died down. The four pigs waited, trembling, with guilt written on every line of their countenances. Napoleon now called upon them to confess their crimes. They were the same four pigs as had protested when Napoleon abolished the Sunday Meetings. Without any further **prompting**⑦ they confessed that they had been secretly in touch with Snowball ever since his expulsion, that they had collaborated with him in destroying the windmill, and that they had entered into an agreement with him to hand over Animal Farm to Mr. Frederick. They added that Snowball had privately admitted to them that he had been Jones's secret agent for years past. When they had finished their confession, the dogs promptly tore their throats out, and in a terrible voice Napoleon demanded whether any other animal had anything to confess.

① spine [spain] *n.* 脊骨
② cower ['kauə] *v.* 蜷缩

③ shriek [ʃriːk] *v.* 尖声叫喊

④ countenance ['kauntənəns]
n. 面部表情
⑤ slunk [slʌŋk]（slink 的过
去式）潜逃

⑥ tumult ['tjuːmʌlt] *n.* 喧闹

⑦ prompting ['prɔmptiŋ] *n.*
敦促

四天后的下午，临近黄昏时，拿破仑命令所有动物在院子里集合。动物们集中起来了之后，拿破仑从住宅里走了出来，身上佩戴着他的那两枚勋章（因为他最近授予自己"一级动物英雄"勋章和"二级动物英雄"勋章），九条狗在他周围蹦来跳去，狂吠着，令所有动物脊椎发冷。他们全都蜷缩在自己所在的位置上，一声不吭，似乎预感到，将要发生什么可怕的事情。

拿破仑神情严肃，站立在那儿注视着自己面前的观众，接着发出了一声尖叫。那些狗立刻向前扑，揪着四头猪的耳朵，拖到了拿破仑的脚下。那些猪又痛苦又恐惧，尖叫着，耳朵鲜血淋漓。狗尝到了血腥味，瞬间疯狂了起来。令每一只动物惊愕不已的是，三条狗扑向拳击手。拳击手见状伸出一只大蹄子，在半空中拦截住一条，把他按倒在地上。那条狗尖叫着求饶，另外两条夹着尾巴逃跑了。拳击手看着拿破仑，想要弄明白是该把狗弄死，还是放开他。拿破仑似乎脸色变了，严厉地喝令拳击手放开狗。拳击手于是抬起蹄子，狗悻悻然离开，身上青一块紫一块的，吠叫着。

不一会儿，喧闹声平息下来了。四头猪等待着，战战兢兢，面部的每一道皱褶里都似乎写满着罪行。拿破仑此时责令他们承认自己的罪行。这四头猪正是当初拿破仑宣布取消星期天"会议"时站出来抗议的那四头。没有等待进一步的催促，他们便承认，雪球遭到驱逐之后，他们同他有过秘密的接触。他们曾配合他一道摧毁风车工程。他们同他达成了协议，决定把动物农场交给弗里德里克先生。他们还补充说，雪球私下里向他们承认，他过去一些年中一直充当琼斯的密探。几头猪承认自己的罪行后，几条狗扑了过去撕破了他们的喉咙。拿破仑声嘶力竭，声音恐怖，质问其他动物是否还有什么要坦白交代的。

The three hens who had been the ringleaders in the attempted rebellion over the eggs now came forward and stated that Snowball had appeared to them in a dream and **incited**① them to disobey Napoleon's orders. They, too, were slaughtered. Then a goose came forward and confessed to having secreted six ears of corn during the last year's harvest and eaten them in the night. Then a sheep confessed to having urinated in the drinking pool urged to do this, so she said, by Snowball, and two other sheep confessed to having murdered an old **ram**②, an especially devoted follower of Napoleon, by chasing him round and round a **bonfire**③ when he was suffering from a cough. They were all **slain**④ on the spot. And so the tale of confessions and executions went on, until there was a pile of **corpses**⑤ lying before Napoleon's feet and the air was heavy with the smell of blood, which had been unknown there since the expulsion of Jones.

When it was all over, the remaining animals, except for the pigs and dogs, crept away in a body. They were shaken and miserable. They did not know which was more shocking—the **treachery**⑥ of the animals who had leagued themselves with Snowball, or the cruel **retribution**⑦ they had just witnessed. In the old days there had often been scenes of bloodshed equally terrible, but it seemed to all of them that it was far worse now that it was happening among themselves. Since Jones had left the farm, until today, no animal had killed another animal. Not even a rat had been killed. They had made their way on to the little knoll where the half-finished windmill stood, and with one accord they all lay down as though **huddling**⑧ together for warmth, Clover, Muriel, Benjamin, the cows, the sheep, and a whole flock of geese and hens, everyone, indeed, except the cat, who had suddenly disappeared just before Napoleon ordered the animals to assemble. For some time nobody spoke. Only Boxer remained on his feet. He **fidgeted**⑨ to and fro, **swishing**⑩ his long black tail against his sides and occasionally uttering a little whinny of surprise. Finally he said:

"I do not understand it. I would not have believed that such things could happen on our farm. It must be due to some fault in ourselves. The solution, as

① incite [in'sait] v. 鼓动

② ram [ræm] n. 公羊

③ bonfire ['bɔn.faiə] n. 篝火

④ slain [slein] slay 的过去分词，宰杀

⑤ corpse [kɔːps] n. 尸体

⑥ treachery ['tretʃəri] n. 背叛

⑦ retribution [.retri'bjuːʃən] n. 惩罚

⑧ huddle ['hʌdl] v. 挤作一团

⑨ fidget ['fidʒit] v. 坐立不安

⑩ swish [swiʃ] v. 嗖地挥动

那三只在那次捍卫鸡蛋未遂行动中领过头的母鸡此时走了出来，陈述说雪球曾经出现在她们的梦境中，怂恿她们违抗拿破仑的命令。她们也遭到了宰杀。紧接着，一只鹅走了出来交代，去年收获季节期间，他私藏了六串谷穗，而且夜间给吃掉了。后来，一只绵羊又交代，曾在饮水池里撒过一泡尿——她说，那是雪球敦促自己这样做的。另外两只绵羊交代说，他们曾设计谋杀了一只老公羊，因为老公羊是拿破仑特别忠实的追随者。老公羊当时咳嗽得厉害，他们追赶着他一圈一圈绕着篝火堆跑。绵羊们立刻全都遭到杀戮。就这样，坦白交代和执行死刑的行动一直在继续着，最后，尸体在拿破仑的跟前堆成了一大堆，空气中弥漫着浓厚的血腥味。这样的情形打从琼斯遭到驱逐之后头一次出现。

这一行动结束之后，除了猪和狗之外，剩下的动物挤成一团，悄然离开了。他们诚惶诚恐，痛苦不堪。他们不知道哪个情况更加丑恶——是那些同雪球相互勾结导致的背叛行为呢，还是他们刚才目睹的残酷惩治。昔日，常常会出现同样恐怖的流血场面，但所有动物都似乎觉得，现在杀戮竟然出现在他们动物之间，这着实要恐怖得多。打从琼斯离开农场以来，时至今日，还没有出现过一只动物杀害另一只的现象。连一只耗子都没有被杀害过。他们一路走向那座小山丘，因为建造了一半的风车矗立在那儿。他们不约而同地躺了下来，好像挤在一块儿取暖似的：苜蓿、穆里尔、本杰明、奶牛、绵羊、整个鹅群、母鸡群，每一只都到齐了，除了那只猫之外——就在拿破仑命令所有动物集合之前，猫突然消失了。好一阵子，动物们谁也没有开口说话。唯有拳击手站立着。他焦躁不安，身子前后摆动着，长长的黑尾巴不停地抽打着身子两侧，还时不时地发出惊讶的叫声。他最后说：

"我对此不理解，简直不相信，这样的事情怎么可能会发生在我们农场？一定是我们自己在什么地方

I see it, is to work harder. From now onwards I shall get up a full hour earlier in the mornings."

And he moved off at his **lumbering**① trot and made for the quarry. Having got there, he collected two successive loads of stone and dragged them down to the windmill before retiring for the night.

The animals huddled about Clover, not speaking. The knoll where they were lying gave them a wide prospect across the countryside. Most of Animal Farm was within their view—the long pasture stretching down to the main road, the hayfield, the spinney, the drinking pool, the ploughed fields where the young wheat was thick and green, and the red roofs of the farm buildings with the smoke curling from the **chimneys**②. It was a clear spring evening. The grass and the bursting hedges were **gilded**③ by the level rays of the sun. Never had the farm and with a kind of surprise they remembered that it was their own farm, every inch of it their own property—appeared to the animals so desirable a place. As Clover looked down the hillside her eyes filled with tears. If she could have spoken her thoughts, it would have been to say that this was not what they had aimed at when they had set themselves years ago to work for the overthrow of the human race. These scenes of terror and slaughter were not what they had looked forward to on that night when old Major first stirred them to rebellion. If she herself had had any picture of the future, it had been of a society of animals set free from hunger and the whip, all equal, each working according to his capacity, the strong protecting the weak, as she had protected the lost brood of ducklings with her foreleg on the night of Major's speech. Instead, she did not know why they had come to a time when no one dared speak his mind, when fierce, growling dogs roamed everywhere, and when you had to watch your comrades torn to pieces after confessing to shocking crimes. There was no thought of rebellion or disobedience in her mind. She knew that, even as things were, they were far better off than they had been in the days of Jones, and that before all else it was needful to prevent the return of the human beings. Whatever happened she would remain faithful, work hard, carry out the orders

① lumbering ['lʌmbəriŋ] a.
笨拙移动的

出了问题。根据我的判断，解决问题的办法就是更加
卖力地干活儿。从现在开始，我每天早晨要提前整一
个小时起床。"

他迈着沉重的步伐离开了，走向采石场。到那儿后，
他连着装了两车石头，拉到了风车建造工地，然后歇息
去了。

动物们依偎在苜蓿周围，缄口不言。他们躺在小
山丘上，前方辽阔的乡野一览无遗，大半座动物农场
尽收眼底——向下延伸到大路的长长牧场、种植着草
料的田地、灌木林、饮水池、翻耕过的长着浓密嫩绿
麦苗的田地、农场上的红色房顶，还有烟囱里冒出的
袅袅炊烟。这是一幅晴朗春日黄昏的景致。落日的余

② chimney ['tʃimni] n. 烟囱
③ gild [gild] v. 使呈金色

晖给草丛和郁郁葱葱的树篱洒上了一抹金色。动物们
惊奇地回想起来了，这是一座原本属于他们自己的农
场，其中的每一寸土地都是他们自己的财产。展示在
动物们面前的农场从未像现在这样，成了他们心中渴
望拥有的地方。苜蓿顺着山坡向下看，眼睛里噙满了
泪水。她若是能够把自己的想法表达出来，那一定会
说，几年前，他们独立自主，为推翻人类而拼命工作。
而眼前的情形并非他们当初想要实现的目标，眼前恐
怖和杀戮的场景也不是老少校第一次鼓励他们奋起反
抗的那天夜晚所憧憬的。她若是对未来有什么展望的
话，那将会是一个属于摆脱了饥饿和皮鞭的动物们的
社会，大家一律平等，每只动物都各尽所能，强者保
护弱者，如同少校发表演讲的那天夜晚她用自己的前
腿保护着那群失散的小鸭那样。相反，她不知道，动
物们怎么会走到这样的地步：任何动物都不敢直抒胸
臆，恶犬狂吠着四处游荡，一些动物同志们坦白交代
了可怕的罪行之后，你只能眼睁睁地看着他们被撕烂。
她的心里并没有反抗或抗命的想法。她知道，即便事
已至此，比起琼斯统治的日子，情况还是要好很多。
现在最重要的是，一定要设法阻止人类卷土重来。不

that were given to her, and accept the leadership of Napoleon. But still, it was not for this that she and all the other animals had hoped and toiled. It was not for this that they had built the windmill and faced the bullets of Jones's gun. Such were her thoughts, though she lacked the words to express them.

At last, feeling this to be in some way a substitute for the words she was unable to find, she began to sing *Beasts of England*. The other animals sitting round her took it up, and they sang it three times over, very tunefully, but slowly and mournfully, in a way they had never sung it before.

They had just finished singing it for the third time when Squealer, attended by two dogs, approached them with the air of having something important to say. He announced that, by a special decree of Comrade Napoleon, *Beasts of England* had been abolished. From now onwards it was forbidden to sing it.

The animals were t**aken aback**[①].

"Why?" cried Muriel.

"It's no longer needed, comrade," said Squealer stiffly. "*Beasts of England* was the song of the Rebellion. But the Rebellion is now completed. The execution of the traitors this afternoon was the final act. The enemy both external and internal has been defeated. In *Beasts of England* we expressed our longing for a better society in days to come. But that society has now been established. Clearly this song has no longer any purpose."

Frightened though they were, some of the animals might possibly have protested, but at this moment the sheep set up their usual bleating of "Four legs good, two legs bad," which went on for several minutes and put an end to the discussion.

So *Beasts of England* was heard no more. In its place Minimus, the poet, had composed another song which began:

Animal Farm, Animal Farm,
Never through me shalt thou come to harm!

管情况如何，她将会一如既往地保持忠诚，卖力干活儿，完成好交给自己的任务，接受拿破仑的领导。但是，尽管如此，她和所有其他动物心中怀有的希望，为之努力干活儿的目标，可不是这个。他们建造风车，直面琼斯的枪射出的子弹，也不是为了这个。这就是她心里面真实的想法，尽管她缺乏言辞来加以表达。

最后，苜蓿觉得自己无法找到合适的言辞来表达，便开始高唱《英格兰的牲畜》。坐在她身边的其他动物们也跟着唱了起来，唱了三遍，声音悦耳动听，但节奏缓慢，韵律悲伤，他们先前从未这样唱过这首歌。

动物们刚刚唱完了第三遍，这时候，尖嗓子在两条狗的护卫下朝着他们走过来了，看架势好像有什么重要的事情。他宣布说，奉了拿破仑同志的特别指令，废除《英格兰的牲畜》。从此，禁止动物们唱这首歌。

动物们大惊失色。

"为什么啊？"穆里尔大声问。

"不再需要这首歌啦，同志们，"尖嗓子说，语气生硬，"《英格兰的牲畜》是反抗运动时期的歌曲。但是，反抗运动现在已经结束了。今天下午对叛徒施行处决是最后的行动。我们已经打败了内外的敌人。《英格兰的牲畜》中表达的是我们对未来更加美好的社会的渴望。但是，那个社会现在已经建立起来了。很显然，这首歌已经没有用途了。"

动物们尽管诚惶诚恐，其中有一些还是可能会提出抗议，但是，就在这个当儿，绵羊们咩咩地念叨起了"四条腿好，两条腿坏"，持续了好几分钟，所以事情无法议论下去了。

至此，动物们再也听不到《英格兰的牲畜》这首歌了。诗人小不点创作了另外一首歌，开头两句是这样的：

> 动物农场，动物农场，
> 我永远不会让你受伤。

① take aback 使吃惊，使惊呆

And this was sung every Sunday morning after the hoisting of the flag. But somehow neither the words nor the tune ever seemed to the animals to **come up to**[①] *Beasts of England.*

① come up to 比得上

这首歌每个星期天早上升旗过后都要唱。但是，不知怎么回事，动物们总是觉得其歌词和旋律都无法同《英格兰的牲畜》的相比。

Chapter VIII

A few days later, when the terror caused by the executions had died down, some of the animals remembered—or thought they remembered that the Sixth Commandment decreed "No animal shall kill any other animal." And though no one cared to mention it in the hearing of the pigs or the dogs, it was felt that the killings which had taken place did not **square with**[①] this. Clover asked Benjamin to read her the Sixth Commandment, and when Benjamin, as usual, said that he refused to **meddle in**[②] such matters, she fetched Muriel. Muriel read the Commandment for her. It ran: "No animal shall kill any other animal *without cause*." **Somehow or other**[③], the last two words had slipped out of the animals' memory. But they saw now that the Commandment had not been violated; for clearly there was good reason for killing the traitors who had leagued themselves with Snowball.

Throughout the year the animals worked even harder than they had worked in the previous year. To rebuild the windmill, with walls twice as thick as before, and to finish it by the appointed date, together with the regular work of the farm, was a tremendous labour. There were times when it seemed to the animals that they worked longer hours and fed no better than they had done in Jones's day. On Sunday mornings Squealer, holding down a long strip of paper with his trotter, would read out to them lists of figures proving that the production of

第八章

几天过后，因杀戮引起的恐慌消散了，一些动物回想起来了——或者觉得他们回想起来了——"七戒"中的第六条明文规定："任何动物都不杀戮别的动物。"尽管他们谁也不想在猪或者狗可能听到的场所提及此事，但他们心里总是觉得，已经发生的诸多杀戮行为与"戒律"不符。苜蓿请求本杰明把"第六条戒律"念给她听，而当本杰明还是和平常一样说自己拒绝掺和此事时，她便去找穆里尔。穆里尔把戒律的内容念给她听了。内容是："任何动物都不得无缘无故杀戮别的动物。"不知什么原因，动物们的记忆中没有"无缘无故"几个字。但是，他们现在明白了，杀戮行为并没有违背"戒律"的规定，因为很显然，叛徒同雪球狼狈为奸，杀戮他们是有充分理由的。

一整年，动物们干活儿比上一年更加卖力。重建风车，墙壁的厚度比先前增加了一倍。要在预定的日期完成工程，农场上的正常活儿照干，这可是巨大的劳动量啊。有些时候，动物们觉得，同琼斯统治的时代相比，他们干活儿的时间更长，吃得反而更糟。每当星期天的早上，尖嗓子就会用蹄子夹着一张长长的

① square with 与……协调或一致

② meddle in 干涉，干预

③ somehow or other 莫名其妙地

every class of foodstuff had increased by two hundred per cent, three hundred per cent, or five hundred per cent, as the case might be. The animals saw no reason to disbelieve him, especially as they could no longer remember very clearly what conditions had been like before the Rebellion. All the same, there were days when they felt that they would sooner have had less figures and more food.

All orders were now issued through Squealer or one of the other pigs. Napoleon himself was not seen in public as often as once in a fortnight. When he did appear, he was attended not only by his **retinue**[1] of dogs but by a black cockerel who marched in front of him and acted as a kind of **trumpeter**[2], letting out a loud "cock-a-doodle-doo" before Napoleon spoke. Even in the farmhouse, it was said, Napoleon inhabited separate apartments from the others. He took his meals alone, with two dogs to wait upon him, and always ate from the Crown Derby dinner service which had been in the glass cupboard in the drawing-room. It was also announced that the gun would be fired every year on Napoleon's birthday, as well as on the other two anniversaries.

Napoleon was now never spoken of simply as "Napoleon." He was always referred to in formal style as "our Leader, Comrade Napoleon," and this pigs liked to invent for him such titles as Father of All Animals, Terror of Mankind, Protector of the Sheep-fold, Ducklings' Friend, **and the like**[3]. In his speeches, Squealer would talk with the tears rolling down his cheeks of Napoleon's wisdom the goodness of his heart, and the deep love he bore to all animals everywhere, even and especially the unhappy animals who still lived in ignorance and slavery on other farms. It had become usual to give Napoleon the credit for every successful achievement and every stroke of good fortune. You would often hear one hen remark to another: "Under the guidance of our Leader, Comrade Napoleon, I have laid five eggs in six days"; or two cows, enjoying a drink at the pool, would exclaim: "Thanks to the leadership of Comrade Napoleon, how excellent this water tastes!" The general feeling on the farm was well expressed in a poem entitled Comrade Napoleon, which was composed by

纸条，向他们宣读一串数字，以此证明，各类饲料产量增加了百分之二百，百分之三百，百分之五百，百分比视情况而定。动物们没有理由不相信他说的话，尤其是，他们不再清楚地记得反抗运动爆发之前的情况如何了。与此同时，他们有时候觉得，宁可数字小一点，饲料多一点。

所有命令现在都是由尖嗓子或者另外某头猪发布的。拿破仑自己则每两个星期公开露面一次。他一旦露面，不仅有恶犬护卫队陪伴，还有一只黑色小公鸡在前面开道，扮演类似于吹号手的角色。拿破仑开口说话之前，小公鸡会响亮地"喔——喔——喔"大叫一通。据说，即便在农场主住宅里，拿破仑也是独居套间，与其他猪分开居住。他独自用餐，由两条狗伺候着他，使用的一直都是先前摆放在客厅玻璃柜中的王冠德比餐具。另外还宣布了：如同另外两个周年纪念日一样，拿破仑每年生日时要鸣枪庆祝。

现在，人们提到拿破仑时，决不能简简单单地称之为"拿破仑"了，而一直都要用正式的称谓，即"我们的领袖拿破仑同志"。那些猪则替他发明创造出了诸如"动物之父""人类的恐惧神""羊圈的守护神""小鸭之友"等等头衔。尖嗓子发表演讲时，总会泪流满面，谈及拿破仑的智慧，其心地如何悲悯善良，对各地的动物如何怀有深切的爱意——特别是对其他农场那些不幸的动物们，因为他们仍然生活在愚昧无知和奴役状态中。每一项成就，每一次好运，都会归功于拿破仑，此事已经成为惯例了。大家常常可以听见一只母鸡对另外一只母鸡说："在我们的领袖拿破仑同志的指引下，我六天当中下了五枚蛋。"或者听见在池塘边美滋滋地喝水的两头奶牛激动地说："多亏有了拿破仑同志的领导，这水喝起来真是甜美啊！"农场上一般动物的感受很充分地体现在一首题为《拿破仑同志》的诗中，诗是小不点写的，内容如下：

① retinue ['retinju:] *n.* 随员
② trumpeter ['trʌmpitə] *n.* 号兵

③ and the like 诸如此类

Minimus and which ran as follows:

> Friend of fatherless!
> Fountain of happiness!
> Lord of the swill-bucket!
> Oh, how my soul is on
> Fire when I gaze at thy
> Calm and commanding eye,
> Like the sun in the sky,
> Comrade Napoleon!
>
> Thou are the giver of
> All that thy creatures love,
> Full belly twice a day, clean straw to roll upon;
> Every beast great or small
> Sleeps at peace in his stall,
> Thou watchest over all,
> Comrade Napoleon!
>
> Had I a sucking-pig,
> Ere he had grown as big
> Even as a pint bottle or as a rolling-pin,
> He should have learned to be
> Faithful and true to thee,
> Yes, his first **squeak**① should be
> "Comrade Napoleon!"

Napoleon approved of this poem and caused it to be inscribed on the wall of the big barn, at the opposite end from the Seven Commandments. It was **surmounted**② by a portrait of Napoleon, in profile, executed by Squealer in

孤儿的朋友!
幸福的源泉!
赐予食物的主啊!
您平静威严的目光,
犹如烈日当空。
啊,每当我凝视着您,
拿破仑同志,
我的心充满了火一般的热情!

您恩赐了
一切生灵所爱的一切。
有一日两顿饱餐,
有洁净的干草打滚躺卧。
每一只牲畜,无论大小,
能够在圈舍里平静入眠。
您守护着一切啊,
拿破仑同志!

我若是有一幼崽,
未及他长大到成年,
即便如奶瓶或擀面杖般大小时,
也要教育他学会对您,
怀有耿耿衷心。
是啊,他的第一声呼喊应该是,
"拿破仑同志!"

① squeak [skwi:k] *n.* 吱吱的
叫声

拿破仑对这首诗倍加赞赏,并责令动物们把它书写
在大谷仓的墙壁上,同"七戒"内容相对应。诗上面用
白色颜料画了一幅拿破仑的侧面肖像。肖像画出自尖嗓
子之手。

② surmount [sə'maunt] *v.* 覆
盖在……顶上

white paint.

Meanwhile, through the agency of Whymper, Napoleon was engaged in complicated negotiations with Frederick and Pilkington. The pile of timber was still unsold. Of the two, Frederick was the more anxious to get hold of it, but he would not offer a reasonable price. At the same time there were renewed rumours that Frederick and his men were plotting to attack Animal Farm and to destroy the windmill, the building of which had aroused furious jealousy in him. Snowball was known to be still **skulking**① on Pinchfield Farm. In the middle of the summer the animals were alarmed to hear that three hens had come forward and confessed that, inspired by Snowball, they had entered into a plot to murder Napoleon. They were executed immediately, and fresh precautions for Napoleon's safety were taken. Four dogs guarded his bed at night, one at each corner, and a young pig named Pinkeye was given the task of tasting all his food before he ate it, lest it should be poisoned.

At about the same time it was given out that Napoleon had arranged to sell the pile of timber to Mr. Pilkington; he was also going to enter into a regular agreement for the exchange of certain products between Animal Farm and Foxwood. The relations between Napoleon and Pilkington, though they were only conducted through Whymper, were now almost friendly. The animals distrusted Pilkington, as a human being, but greatly preferred him to Frederick, whom they both feared and hated. As the summer wore on, and the windmill neared completion, the rumours of an **impending**② **treacherous**③ attack grew stronger and stronger. Frederick, it was said, intended to bring against them twenty men all armed with guns, and he had already bribed the **magistrates**④ and police, so that if he could once get hold of the title-deeds of Animal Farm they would ask no questions. Moreover, terrible stories were leaking out from Pinchfield about the cruelties that Frederick practised upon his animals. He had **flogged**⑤ an old horse to death, he starved his cows, he had killed a dog by throwing it into the **furnace**⑥, he amused himself in the evenings by making cocks fight with **splinters**⑦ of razor-blade tied to their **spurs**⑧. The animals' blood boiled with

① skulk [skʌlk] v. 躲藏

与此同时，通过中间人温佩尔牵线搭桥，拿破仑同弗里德里克和皮尔金顿进行了一次次复杂的谈判，那一堆木料尚未成交。两个人当中，弗里德里克更加迫不及待想要购买木料，但是，他出的价钱不合理。同时，又出现了新的传闻，说弗里德里克和他的雇员正在密谋对动物农场发起攻击，想要摧毁风车工程，因为建造风车的事情已经令他心里酸溜溜的。据说雪球仍然藏匿在窄地农场。仲夏时节，动物们诚惶诚恐，听到三只母鸡主动坦白交代说，她们受到雪球的蛊惑，参与了一场旨在谋杀拿破仑的阴谋。三只母鸡立刻被处决了。为了保护拿破仑的安全，动物们采取了新的安保措施。四条狗夜间守护在他的床边，每条狗守住一个角。有头名叫粉红眼的小猪接受了一项任务，即但凡拿破仑要吃的东西，粉红眼都要先品尝一番，防止食物被下过毒。

大概在同一时间，动物们得到了通知，说拿破仑已经安排好了，准备把那堆木料卖给皮尔金顿先生。他还打算签订一份长期协议，拟在动物农场和狐狸林农场之间就某些产品进行交换。拿破仑和皮尔金顿之间虽说只是通过温佩尔建立关系的，但他们的关系现在几乎可以说是很友好了。作为人类，动物们信不过皮尔金顿，但是，相对于他们既害怕又仇视的弗里德里克，他们还是更加愿意同皮尔金顿打交道。夏季慢慢过去，风车工程接近竣工了。风声越来越紧，动物们纷纷传言说，弗里德里克即将对农场发起一次恶意袭击。据说，他打算率领二十个人，荷枪实弹地对付他们，而且已经买通了地方治安官和警察，一旦他拿到了农场的地契，那些人便会对此事不闻不问。此外，各种可怕的说法也从窄地农场传出，说弗里德里克如何对自己的动物施暴。他曾用鞭子抽打一匹老马，导致其死亡；他让奶牛们忍饥挨饿；他把一条狗扔进炉膛里烧死；傍晚时分，他把剃刀片绑在公鸡的爪子上，让他们互相打斗，以此来取乐。动物们听到自己的同志受到如此这般的虐待，怒火中烧，热

② impending [im'pendiŋ] a. 即将发生的
③ treacherous ['tretʃərəs] a. 奸诈的
④ magistrate ['mædʒistreit] n. 地方官员

⑤ flog [flɔg] v. 鞭打
⑥ furnace ['fɜːnis] n. 熔炉

⑦ splinter ['splintə] n. 裂片
⑧ spur [spɜː] n. 踢马刺，靴刺

rage when they heard of these things being done to their comrades, and sometimes they **clamoured**① to be allowed to go out in a body and attack Pinchfield Farm, drive out the humans, and set the animals free. But Squealer counselled them to avoid **rash actions**② and trust in Comrade Napoleon's strategy.

Nevertheless, feeling against Frederick continued to run high. One Sunday morning Napoleon appeared in the barn and explained that he had never at any time contemplated selling the pile of timber to Frederick; he considered it beneath his dignity, he said, to have dealings with **scoundrels**③ of that description. The pigeons who were still sent out to spread tidings of the Rebellion were forbidden to set foot anywhere on Foxwood, and were also ordered to drop their former slogan of "Death to Humanity" in favour of "Death to Frederick." In the late summer yet another of Snowball's **machinations**④ was laid bare. The wheat crop was full of weeds, and it was discovered that on one of his **nocturnal**⑤ visits Snowball had mixed weed seeds with the seed corn. A **gander**⑥ who had been **privy**⑦ to the plot had confessed his guilt to Squealer and immediately committed suicide by swallowing deadly **nightshade**⑧ **berries**⑨. The animals now also learned that Snowball had never as many of them had believed hitherto received the order of "Animal Hero First Class." This was merely a legend which had been spread some time after the Battle of the Cowshed by Snowball himself. So far from being decorated, he had been **censured**⑩ for showing **cowardice**⑪ in the battle. Once again some of the animals heard this with a certain bewilderment, but Squealer was soon able to convince them that their memories had been at fault.

In the autumn, by a tremendous, exhausting effort for the harvest had to be gathered at almost the same time the windmill was finished. The machinery had still to be installed, and Whymper was negotiating the purchase of it, but the structure was completed. In the teeth of every difficulty, in spite of inexperience, of primitive implements, of bad luck and of Snowball's treachery, the work had been finished punctually to the very day! Tired out but proud, the animals walked round and round their masterpiece, which appeared even more beautiful in their eyes than when it had been built the first time. Moreover, the walls were

血沸腾。有时候，他们大声嚷嚷着，请求允许倾巢出动，对窄地农场发起进攻，驱逐人类，让那儿的动物获得自由。但是，尖嗓子劝说他们不要鲁莽行事，要相信拿破仑同志的战略战术。

然而，反对弗里德里克的情绪依然持续高涨。一个星期天的上午，拿破仑出现在大谷仓，向大家解释说，他任何时候都没有考虑要把那堆木料卖给弗里德里克。他说，同那样的无赖货色进行交易，有损自己的尊严。那些被派遣出去散布要爆发反抗运动消息的鸽子禁止涉足狐狸林农场的任何地方。他们接到传令，把先前"消灭人类"的口号改为"消灭弗里德里克"。到了夏末，他们还揭穿了雪球的另一次阴谋。麦地里杂草丛生，动物们弄清楚了，雪球有一次夜间潜入农场时，在麦种里掺入了野草籽。有只公鹅曾经参与了这一阴谋，他向尖嗓子坦白交代了自己的罪行后便立刻吞食毒浆果自杀身亡了。动物们现在还得知，雪球并非像他们中许多成员至今仍然相信的那样得过什么"一级动物英雄"勋章。这事纯属传说，是"牛棚之战"过后不久雪球自己传播扩散的。他不仅根本没有被授予勋章，而且还因为在战斗中的懦弱表现受到了大众的谴责。一些动物听到这个情况之后，还是显得迷惑不解，但是，尖嗓子很快便说服了他们，让他们相信是自己的记忆力出了问题。

秋天到了，动物们竭尽全力，艰苦劳作，因为他们完成风车建造工程的同时，还必须要抢收庄稼。不过，机械设备还有待安装，温佩尔正在协商购置事宜，但主体结构已经完成了。动物们面对着每一个困难，尽管缺乏经验，设备落后，运气不佳，雪球背叛，但他们还是如期完成了工程！动物们精疲力竭，但倍感自豪。他们绕着自己的杰作走了一圈又一圈。在他们看来，风车工程甚至比第一次建造得还要更加完美。此外，墙体的厚度比先前增加了一倍。这一次，除非使用炸药，否则任

① clamour ['klæmə] v. 吵闹着要求

② rash action 冒失的行为

③ scoundrel ['skaundrəl] n. 恶棍，无赖

④ machination [,mæki'neiʃən] n. 阴谋
⑤ nocturnal [nɔk'tɔːnəl] a. 夜间的
⑥ gander ['gændə] n. 雄鹅
⑦ privy ['privi] a. 暗中参与的
⑧ nightshade ['nait,ʃeid] n. 茄属植物
⑨ berry ['beri] n. 浆果

⑩ censure ['senʃə] v. 谴责
⑪ cowardice ['kauədis] n. 懦弱

twice as thick as before. Nothing short of explosives would lay them low this time! And when they thought of how they had laboured, what discouragements they had overcome, and the enormous difference that would be made in their lives when the sails were turning and the dynamos running—when they thought of all this, their tiredness **forsook**① them and they **gambolled**② round and round the windmill, uttering cries of triumph. Napoleon himself, attended by his dogs and his cockerel, came down to inspect the completed work; he personally congratulated the animals on their achievement, and announced that the mill would be named Napoleon Mill.

Two days later the animals were called together for a special meeting in the barn. They were struck dumb with surprise when Napoleon announced that he had sold the pile of timber to Frederick. Tomorrow Frederick's wagons would arrive and begin carting it away. Throughout the whole period of his seeming friendship with Pilkington, Napoleon had really been in secret agreement with Frederick.

All relations with Foxwood had been broken off; insulting messages had been sent to Pilkington. The pigeons had been told to avoid Pinchfield Farm and to alter their slogan from "Death to Frederick" to "Death to Pilkington." At the same time Napoleon assured the animals that the stories of an impending attack on Animal Farm were completely untrue, and that the tales about Frederick's cruelty to his own animals had been greatly exaggerated. All these rumours had probably originated with Snowball and his agents. It now appeared that Snowball was not, after all, hiding on Pinchfield Farm, and in fact had never been there in his life: he was living in considerable luxury, so it was said at Foxwood, and had in reality been a **pensioner**③ of Pilkington for years past.

The pigs were **in ecstasies**④ over Napoleon's cunning. By seeming to be friendly with Pilkington he had forced Frederick to raise his price by twelve pounds. But the superior quality of Napoleon's mind, said Squealer, was shown in the fact that he trusted nobody, not even Frederick. Frederick had wanted to pay for the timber with something called a cheque, which, it seemed, was

何东西都摧毁不了它。动物们想到自己付出了怎样的艰辛劳动，克服了怎样的困难挫折；他们想到风车的翼板一旦转动起来，发电机运转起来，他们的生活将会发生怎样的变化——每当想到这一切时，他们的疲劳便会顿时消失。他们便会一圈又一圈地绕着风车欢跳嬉戏，嘴里不停地发出胜利的呼喊。拿破仑在他那一群狗和那只小公鸡的簇拥下，亲临现场视察竣工的工程。他为动物们取得的成就向他们表示祝贺，并且宣布，风车拟命名为"拿破仑风车"。

① forsook [fɔ:'suk]（forsake 的过去式）v. 抛弃
② gambol ['gæmbəl] v. 跳蹦

两天过后，动物们被召集到大谷仓召开一次特别会议。拿破仑在会上宣布，他已经把那一堆木料卖给了弗里德里克。动物们听后惊得目瞪口呆。翌日，弗里德里克便会派车过来把木料运走。整个这段时期内，拿破仑同皮尔金顿之间貌似关系融洽，但他暗地里却同弗里德里克达成了协议。

动物农场断绝了同狐狸林农场的一切关系，给皮尔金顿寄去了带有侮辱性的信件。鸽子们得到了吩咐，要避开窄地农场，把他们的口号由"消灭弗里德里克"改为"消灭皮尔金顿"。与此同时，拿破仑向动物们保证说，有关动物农场即将遭到袭击的传言纯属子虚乌有，有关弗里德里克虐待自己的动物的说法也是夸大其词，上述种种传言很可能源于雪球和他的同谋。现在看起来，雪球压根儿就没有藏匿在窄地农场。事实上，他压根就没有涉足过那儿。大家纷纷传言，说他一直住在狐狸林农场，过着相当奢华的生活。过去一些年中，实际上一直由皮尔金顿供养着。

③ pensioner ['penʃənə] n. 受豢养者
④ in ecstasy 兴奋不已

拿破仑足智多谋，所有猪都为之欣喜若狂。他表面上维持同皮尔金顿的友好关系，迫使弗里德里克把购买木料的价格提升了十二英镑。但是，尖嗓子说，体现拿破仑非凡智慧的还有这样一个事实：他谁都信不过，即便对弗里德里克也罢。弗里德里克想要用一种叫作支票的东西来支付购买木料的款项。看起来，那支票只是一

a piece of paper with a promise to pay written upon it. But Napoleon was too clever for him. He had demanded payment in real five-pound notes, which were to be handed over before the timber was removed. Already Frederick had paid up; and the sum he had paid was just enough to buy the machinery for the windmill.

Meanwhile the timber was being carted away at high speed. When it was all gone, another special meeting was held in the barn for the animals to inspect Frederick's bank-notes. Smiling **beatifically**[1], and wearing both his decorations, Napoleon **reposed**[2] on a bed of straw on the platform, with the money at his side, neatly piled on a china dish from the farmhouse kitchen. The animals filed slowly past, and each gazed his fill. And Boxer put out his nose to sniff at the bank-notes, and the **flimsy**[3] white things stirred and rustled in his breath.

Three days later there was a terrible **hullabaloo**[4]. Whymper, his face deadly pale, came racing up the path on his bicycle, flung it down in the yard and rushed straight into the farmhouse. The next moment a choking roar of rage sounded from Napoleon's apartments. The news of what had happened sped round the farm like wildfire. The banknotes were **forgeries**[5]! Frederick had got the timber for nothing!

Napoleon called the animals together immediately and in a terrible voice pronounced the death sentence upon Frederick. When captured, he said, Frederick should be boiled alive. At the same time he warned them that after this treacherous deed the worst was to be expected. Frederick and his men might make their long-expected attack at any moment. **Sentinels**[6] were placed at all the approaches to the farm. In addition, four pigeons were sent to Foxwood with a **conciliatory**[7] message, which it was hoped might reestablish good relations with Pilkington.

The very next morning the attack came. The animals were at breakfast when the look-outs came racing in with the news that Frederick and his followers had already come through the five-barred gate. Boldly enough the animals **sallied**[8]

张纸而已，上面写着承诺付款的数字。但聪明如拿破仑，才不会上他的当呢。他要求木料运走之前，便要拿到一张张五英镑面额的现钞。弗里德里克已经付清钱款，数额足够用来购置风车所需的机械设备。

期间，木料被迅速运走了。这件事情处理完毕之后，动物们再次聚集在大谷仓召开一次特别会议，查看一番弗里德里克支付的那些钞票。拿破仑满脸微笑，神采奕奕，身上佩戴着他的那两枚勋章，躺卧在台子上那堆干草铺成的床上，钱放在他身边，整整齐齐地码在从厨房拿来的一只空瓷盘上。动物们排成队伍缓步走过，挨个盯着钞票看。拳击手伸长着鼻子嗅了嗅那钞票，他的鼻息把那又薄又白的玩意儿吹拂得抖动了起来，发出轻微的簌簌声。

三天过后，出现了一场可怕的骚乱。温佩尔脸色煞白，骑着自行车沿着小道急速赶来，把自行车往院里一扔，便直接冲向农场主住宅。少顷，拿破仑的套房里传来气急败坏的怒吼声。事情很快便犹如野火一般蔓延开了。钞票是假的！弗里德里克竟然没有花费分文便运走了那堆木料！

拿破仑立刻把动物们召集到了一块儿，宣布判处弗里德里克死刑，声音恐怖。他说，一旦逮住了弗里德里克，便要把他活活煮了。与此同时，他还提醒动物们，有了这种背信弃义的行为之后，还会有更加恶劣的行为发生。弗里德里克和他的雇员随时都有可能发起蓄谋已久的袭击。动物们在通向农场的路口都设置了岗哨。此外，他们还派出了四只鸽子前往狐狸林农场，带去了一封和解信，信中表达了同皮尔金顿重续友好关系的愿望。

就在翌日早晨，敌人果然发起了进攻。动物们正在用早餐，突然，岗哨上的哨兵跑了过来，报告说，弗里德里克领着一帮人已经冲过了五道门闩的大门。动物们英勇无畏，即刻出发迎战。但是，这一次，他们并没有

① beatifically [ˌbiːəˈtifikli] *ad.* 快乐地
② repose [riˈpəuz] *v.* 躺着休息

③ flimsy [ˈflimzi] *a.* 轻而薄的
④ hullabaloo [ˌhʌləbəˈluː] *n.* 喧嚣

⑤ forgery [ˈfɔːdʒəri] *n.* 伪造品

⑥ sentinel [ˈsentinəl] *n.* 哨兵
⑦ conciliatory [kənˈsiliətəri] *a.* 调解的

⑧ sally [ˈsæli] *v.* 动身

forth to meet them, but this time they did not have the easy victory that they had had in the Battle of the Cowshed. There were fifteen men, with half a dozen guns between them, and they opened fire as soon as they got within fifty yards. The animals could not face the terrible explosions and the **stinging**① pellets, and in spite of the efforts of Napoleon and Boxer to rally them, they were soon driven back. A number of them were already wounded. They took **refuge**② in the farm buildings and **peeped**③ cautiously out from **chinks**④ and knot-holes. The whole of the big pasture, including the windmill, was in the hands of the enemy. For the moment even Napoleon seemed at a loss. He paced up and down without a word, his tail rigid and twitching. **Wistful**⑤ glances were sent in the direction of Foxwood. If Pilkington and his men would help them, the day might yet be won. But at this moment the four pigeons, who had been sent out on the day before, returned, one of them bearing a scrap of paper from Pilkington. On it was pencilled the words: **"Serves you right**⑥**."**

Meanwhile Frederick and his men had halted about the windmill. The animals watched them, and a murmur of dismay went round. Two of the men had produced a **crowbar**⑦ and a **sledgehammer**⑧. They were going to knock the windmill down.

"Impossible!" cried Napoleon. "We have built the walls far too thick for that. They could not knock it down in a week. Courage, comrades!"

But Benjamin was watching the movements of the men intently. The two with the hammer and the crowbar were drilling a hole near the base of the windmill. Slowly, and with an air almost of amusement, Benjamin nodded his long **muzzle**⑨.

"I thought so," he said. "Do you not see what they are doing? In another moment they are going to pack blasting powder into that hole."

Terrified, the animals waited. It was impossible now to venture out of the shelter of the buildings. After a few minutes the men were seen to be running in all directions. Then there was a deafening roar. The pigeons **swirled**⑩ into the air, and all the animals, except Napoleon, flung themselves flat on their bellies

① stinging ['stiŋiŋ] *a.* 刺人的

② refuge ['refjuːdʒ] *n.* 避难
③ peep [piːp] *v.* 偷看
④ chink [tʃiŋk] *n.* 裂缝

⑤ wistful ['wistful] *a.* 渴望的

⑥ serve someone right 给某人应得的惩罚
⑦ crowbar ['krəu,bɑː] *n.* 撬棍
⑧ sledgehammer ['sledʒ,hæmə] *n.* 大锤

⑨ muzzle ['mʌzl] *n.*（狗、马等的）鼻口部

⑩ swirl [swəːl] *v.* 盘绕

像当初"牛棚之战"时的情形一样，轻而易举取得胜利。对方来了十五个人，带了有五六支枪。他们在五十码开外处便开枪射击。动物们无法抵挡住一阵阵枪击和引起灼痛的子弹。尽管拿破仑和拳击手费了很大的力气才鼓起了他们的士气，但很快又被击退了。很多动物已经负伤了，他们躲避到了农场的窝棚里，小心翼翼地对着缝隙和小孔朝外看。敌人占领了整个一片大牧场，包括风车在内。一时间，连拿破仑似乎都不知道该怎么办了。他缄口不言，来回踱着步，尾巴僵硬，不停地摆动着。他一次次地朝着狐狸林农场的方向看，目光中满怀着期望。皮尔金顿和他的雇员若是能够助他们一臂之力，今天的战斗或许可以取胜。但是，就在这个当儿，头天派出去的四只鸽子返回了，其中的一只衔着皮尔金顿写来的一张字条。上面用铅笔写着："你们咎由自取。"

这时候，弗里德里克和他雇员们停在风车四周。动物们一面注视着他们，一面绝望地小声议论起来。其中两个人拿出一根钢钎和一把大铁锤，他们准备捣毁风车。

"不可能！"拿破仑说，"我们建筑的墙壁可厚实啦，捣毁不了的，即便耗时一个星期也捣毁不了。鼓起勇气来，同志们！"

但是，本杰明聚精会神地注视着那些人的举动。那两个拿着大铁锤和钢钎的人正在风车底部的墙体上打洞。本杰明点了点自己长长的头部，动作缓慢，那样子好像觉得挺有趣。

"我就想到了这一着，"他说，"你们没有看见他们在干什么吗？片刻之后，他们就会往凿开的洞里塞炸药呢。"

动物们惊恐万状，等待着。他们现在不可能冒险走出窝棚的隐蔽处。几分钟过后，他们便看见那些人朝着四面八方奔跑。然后便是一声震耳欲聋的巨响。鸽子们盘旋着飞向空中，除了拿破仑之外，所有动物全都直挺

and hid their faces. When they got up again, a huge cloud of black smoke was hanging where the windmill had been. Slowly the breeze drifted it away. The windmill had ceased to exist!

At this sight the animals' courage returned to them. The fear and despair they had felt a moment earlier were drowned in their rage against this **vile**①, **contemptible**② act. A mighty cry for **vengeance**③ went up, and without waiting for further orders they charged forth in a body and made straight for the enemy. This time they did not heed the cruel pellets that swept over them like **hail**④. It was a savage, bitter battle. The men fired again and again, and, when the animals got to close quarters, lashed out with their sticks and their heavy boots. A cow, three sheep, and two geese were killed, and nearly everyone was wounded. Even Napoleon, who was directing operations from the rear, had the tip of his tail **chipped**⑤ by a pellet. But the men did not go **unscathed**⑥ either. Three of them had their heads broken by blows from Boxer's hoofs; another was gored in the belly by a cow's horn; another had his trousers nearly torn off by Jessie and Bluebell. And when the nine dogs of Napoleon's own bodyguard, whom he had instructed to make a **detour**⑦ under cover of the hedge, suddenly appeared on the men's **flank**⑧, baying ferociously, panic overtook them. They saw that they were in danger of being surrounded. Frederick shouted to his men to get out while the going was good, and the next moment the cowardly enemy was running for dear life. The animals chased them right down to the bottom of the field, and got in some last kicks at them as they forced their way through the thorn hedge.

They had won, but they were weary and bleeding. Slowly they began to **limp**⑨ back towards the farm. The sight of their dead comrades stretched upon the grass moved some of them to tears. And for a little while they halted in sorrowful silence at the place where the windmill had once stood. Yes, it was gone; almost the last trace of their labour was gone! Even the foundations were partially destroyed. And in rebuilding it they could not this time, as before, make use of the fallen stones. This time the stones had vanished too. The force of the

挺地趴在地上，肚子朝下，把脸部藏了起来。当他们重新站立起来时，风车所在地的上方笼罩着一团黑烟似的乌云。慢慢地，微风吹散了乌云，但风车已经不复存在了！

面对此情此景，动物们恢复了勇气。他们片刻之前怀有的恐惧和绝望淹没在眼前卑鄙可耻的行径引起的愤怒之中了，顿时响起了要报仇雪恨的巨大呐喊。动物们没有等到再下达命令便行动一致，直接向敌人发起了进攻。这一次，他们不再理会那犹如冰雹一般从他们身边呼啸而过的子弹。这是一场野蛮而又惨烈的战斗。那些人一次又一次地开枪射击，等到动物们同他们的距离很接近时，他们便挥动着棍子抽打，用沉重的靴子猛踢。一头奶牛、三只绵羊和两只鹅阵亡了，几乎每一只动物都受了伤，连处在队伍后面负责指挥的拿破仑，其尾巴尖都被子弹削掉了一小块。但是，那伙人也并非毫发无损。三个人被拳击手的蹄子踢破了脑袋；还有个人被一头奶牛的角顶破了肚皮；另外有个人差点被杰西和蓝铃把裤子给扯掉了。那九条贴身护卫拿破仑的狗奉命凭借树篱的掩护迂回包抄过去。狗突然出现在那些人一侧，面目狰狞，厉声狂吠。他们吓得魂飞魄散。他们看出来了，自己正处于被包围的险境之中。弗里德里克冲着手下人大喊，趁着还来得及赶紧逃跑。紧接着，胆怯的敌人便开始夺路逃命了。动物们奋力追赶，一直追到了田地的尽头。那些人强行从荆棘篱笆处逃跑时，动物们还最后踢了他们几蹄子。

动物们取得了胜利，但他们疲惫不堪，鲜血直流。慢慢地，他们开始一瘸一拐地返回农场。看到阵亡的同志们的遗体躺卧在草地上，有些动物触景生情，流下了眼泪。好一阵子，他们伫立在风车的所在地，情绪悲伤，默不作声。是啊，风车没有了，他们艰辛劳作，连最后的一点痕迹都没有留下，连地基都毁掉了一些。这一次，他们若是要重建风车工程，不可能像先前那样利用得上坍塌的石料；这一次石块也消失不见了，爆炸的冲力把

---

① vile [vail] *a.* 卑鄙的
② contemptible [kən'temptəbl] *a.* 可鄙的
③ vengeance ['vendʒəns] *n.* 报复
④ hail [heil] *n.* 冰雹

⑤ chip [tʃip] *v.* 削
⑥ unscathed [ʌn'skeiðd] *a.* 未受伤的

⑦ detour ['diːtuə] *n.* 绕道
⑧ flank [flæŋk] *n.* 侧面

⑨ limp [limp] *v.* 跛行

explosion had flung them to distances of hundreds of yards. It was as though the windmill had never been.

As they approached the farm Squealer, who had unaccountably been absent during the fighting, came skipping towards them, whisking his tail and beaming with satisfaction. And the animals heard, from the direction of the farm buildings, the solemn booming of a gun.

"What is that gun firing for?" said Boxer.

"To celebrate our victory!" cried Squealer.

"What victory?" said Boxer. His knees were bleeding, he had lost a shoe and split his hoof, and a dozen pellets had **lodged**① themselves in his hind leg.

"What victory, comrade? Have we not driven the enemy off our soil—the sacred soil of Animal Farm?"

"But they have destroyed the windmill. And we had worked on it for two years!"

"What matter? We will build another windmill. We will build six windmills if we feel like it. You do not appreciate, comrade, the mighty thing that we have done. The enemy was in occupation of this very ground that we stand upon. And now, thanks to the leadership of Comrade Napoleon, we have won every inch of it back again!"

"Then we have won back what we had before," said Boxer.

"That is our victory," said Squealer.

They limped into the yard. The pellets under the skin of Boxer's leg **smarted**② painfully. He saw ahead of him the heavy labour of rebuilding the windmill from the foundations, and already in imagination he **braced himself**③ for the task. But for the first time it occurred to him that he was eleven years old and that perhaps his great muscles were not quite what they had once been.

But when the animals saw the green flag flying, and heard the gun firing again—seven times it was fired in all and heard the speech that Napoleon made, congratulating them on their conduct, it did seem to them after all that they had won a great victory. The animals slain in the battle were given a solemn funeral.

石块冲到了几百码之外的地方。此处好像从未有过风车一样。

战斗中，尖嗓子莫名其妙地不见了。他们快要进入农场时，他却蹦蹦跳跳地迎上前来，不停地摇着尾巴，一副春风得意的样子。动物们听见从农场窝棚的方向传来了用作礼炮的枪声。

"鸣枪干什么啊？"拳击手问了一声。

"庆祝胜利呀！"尖嗓子大声说。

"什么胜利？"拳击手说，他的膝盖仍然鲜血淋漓。他丢失了一块马蹄铁，蹄子裂开了，后腿部足足中了一打子弹。

"什么胜利，同志们？我们难道没有把敌人从我们的土地上——动物农场神圣的土地上赶跑吗？"

"但是，敌人炸毁了风车。我们千辛万苦干了两年呢！"

"这算得了什么？我们可以再建造一座风车。只要我们愿意，我们可以建造六座风车。同志啊，你并没有充分领悟到，我们干了一件多么了不起的事情呀。敌人曾经占据着我们脚下的这一片土地。而现如今，多亏有了拿破仑同志的领导，我们这才夺回了每一寸土地！"

"这么说来，我们赢回了曾经拥有过的东西啦？"拳击手说。

"这是我们的胜利啊！"尖嗓子说。

他们一瘸一拐地进入了院落。拳击手中了枪弹的那条腿疼痛不已。要在地基上重建风车，他看到了摆在自己面前的艰辛劳动，心里面已经接受了那项任务了。但是，他突然第一次意识到，自己已经十一岁了，身子骨恐怕今非昔比了。

但是，动物们看见绿色旗帜飘扬着，再次听见了鸣枪的声音——总共鸣了七枪，听到了拿破仑发表的演讲，祝贺他们在战斗中的表现。这时候，他们确实觉得，自己取得了一次了不起的胜利。他们为战斗中阵亡的动

① lodge [lɒdʒ] v. 嵌入

② smart [smɑːt] v.（伤口）疼痛

③ brace oneself 做好准备

·135·

Boxer and Clover pulled the wagon which served as a **hearse**①, and Napoleon himself walked at the head of the **procession**②. Two whole days were given over to celebrations. There were songs, speeches, and more firing of the gun, and a special gift of an apple was bestowed on every animal, with two ounces of corn for each bird and three biscuits for each dog. It was announced that the battle would be called the Battle of the Windmill, and that Napoleon had created a new decoration, the Order of the Green Banner, which he had conferred upon himself. In the general **rejoicings**③ the unfortunate affair of the banknotes was forgotten.

It was a few days later than this that the pigs came upon a case of whisky in the cellars of the farmhouse. It had been **overlooked**④ at the time when the house was first occupied. That night there came from the farmhouse the sound of loud singing, in which, to everyone's surprise, the strains of *Beasts of England* were mixed up. At about half past nine Napoleon, wearing an old bowler hat of Mr. Jones's, was distinctly seen to emerge from the back door, gallop rapidly round the yard, and disappear indoors again. But in the morning a deep silence hung over the farmhouse. Not a pig appeared to be stirring. It was nearly nine o'clock when Squealer made his appearance, walking slowly and **dejectedly**⑤, his eyes dull, his tail hanging limply behind him, and with every appearance of being seriously ill. He called the animals together and told them that he had a terrible piece of news to impart. Comrade Napoleon was dying!

A cry of **lamentation**⑥ went up. Straw was laid down outside the doors of the farmhouse, and the animals walked on tiptoe. With tears in their eyes they asked one another what they should do if their Leader were taken away from them. A rumour went round that Snowball had after all **contrived**⑦ to introduce poison into Napoleon's food. At eleven o'clock Squealer came out to make another announcement. As his last act upon earth, Comrade Napoleon had pronounced a solemn decree: the drinking of alcohol was to be punished by death.

By the evening, however, Napoleon appeared to be somewhat better, and the following morning Squealer was able to tell them that he was well on the

① hearse [həːs] *n.* 灵车
② procession [prəuˈseʃən] *n.* 队伍

③ rejoicing [riˈdʒɔisiŋ] *n.* 欣喜

④ overlook [ˌəuvəˈluk] *v.* 忽略

⑤ dejectedly [diˈdʒektidli] *ad.* 沮丧地

⑥ lamentation [ˌlæmenˈteiʃən] *n.* 哀伤

⑦ contrive [kənˈtraiv] *v.* 图谋

物举行了庄严的葬礼。拳击手和苜蓿拉着用作灵车的大车，拿破仑本人则行走在送葬队伍的最前头。各种庆祝活动接连进行了整整两天。动物们又是唱歌又是演讲，还鸣了更多礼炮，每只动物都领到了一个苹果，作为特殊的礼物。每只禽类领到了两盎司谷物，每条狗领到了三块饼干。已经宣布了，这次战斗命名为"风车之战"。拿破仑设计出了一枚新的勋章——"绿色旗帜勋章"。他把勋章授予了自己。大家都沉浸在一片喜庆之中，因此，忘掉了那件钞票的倒霉事。

数日过后，那些猪在农场主住宅的地窖里偶然发现了一箱威士忌酒。他们刚刚搬进住宅时并没有注意到有酒。当天夜晚，住宅里传出嘹亮的歌声。令动物们感到惊讶的是，他们竟然听见了其中蕴含着《英格兰的牲畜》的旋律。约莫九点半钟光景，动物们清楚地看见拿破仑头戴一顶当初琼斯先生的圆顶旧礼帽从后门外出，绕着院落快速奔跑，然后又返回室内不见了。但是，翌日早晨，住宅内一片寂静，看不见任何猪的活动。已经将近九点钟了，尖嗓子这才露面，步伐缓慢地行走着，神情沮丧，目光呆滞，尾巴软绵绵地耷拉在屁股后面，一副病得很严重的样子。他把动物们召集到一块儿，对大家说，他要告诉大家一个十分沉痛的消息：拿破仑同志生命垂危！

动物当中响起了一阵悲痛的号哭。农场主住宅几扇门外面铺上了干草，动物们行走时踮着蹄子。他们的眼中噙满了泪水，彼此问对方，如若他们的领袖离他们而去了，他们该怎么办。有传言说，雪球一直在想方设法往拿破仑的食物中下毒。上午十一点钟时，尖嗓子从室内出来第二次通报。作为拿破仑同志在世间做的最后一件事情，他发出了一道庄严的指令：凡饮酒者要处以死刑。

不过，到了傍晚时分，拿破仑的情况似乎有所好转。翌日早晨，尖嗓子告诉动物们，拿破仑同志正在康复中。

way to recovery. By the evening of that day Napoleon was back at work, and on the next day it was learned that he had instructed Whymper to purchase in Willingdon some booklets on **brewing**① and **distilling**②. A week later Napoleon gave orders that the small paddock beyond the orchard, which it had previously been intended to set aside as a grazing-ground for animals who were past work, was to be ploughed up. It was given out that the pasture was exhausted and needed reseeding; but it soon became known that Napoleon intended to sow it with barley.

About this time there occurred a strange incident which hardly anyone was able to understand. One night at about twelve o'clock there was a loud crash in the yard, and the animals rushed out of their stalls. It was a moonlit night. At the foot of the end wall of the big barn, where the Seven Commandments were written, there lay a ladder broken in two pieces. Squealer, temporarily stunned, was sprawling beside it, and near at hand there lay a lantern, a paint-brush, and an overturned pot of white paint. The dogs immediately made a ring round Squealer, and **escorted**③ him back to the farmhouse as soon as he was able to walk. None of the animals could form any idea as to what this meant, except old Benjamin, who nodded his muzzle with a knowing air, and seemed to understand, but would say nothing.

But a few days later Muriel, reading over the Seven Commandments to herself, noticed that there was yet another of them which the animals had remembered wrong. They had thought the Fifth Commandment was "No animal shall drink alcohol," but there were two words that they had forgotten. Actually the Commandment read: "No animal shall drink alcohol *to excess.*"

到了当天傍晚，拿破仑返回到工作岗位了。又过了一天，大家得知，他已经嘱咐温佩尔去威灵登购买一些关于酿酒①和蒸馏②的小册子了。一个星期过后，拿破仑发布命令，果园那边那片小牧场现在拟进行耕作，那儿先前是预留给丧失了劳动能力的动物作草场用的。动物们接到了通知，那片牧场已经枯萎了，需要重新播撒草籽。但是，动物们很快便知道，拿破仑打算在牧场上种植大麦。

大概就在那期间，发生了一件不可思议的事情，几乎所有动物都难以理解。一天夜里十二点钟的样子，院落传来一声巨响，动物们冲出了窝棚。夜晚月光皎洁。在大谷仓一端那面写着"七戒"条文的墙壁下，横着一张断成两截的梯子。尖嗓子躺在梯子旁边，一时昏厥过去了。他旁边有一盏提灯、一把刷子，还有一瓶打翻的白色颜料。那些狗立刻把尖嗓子给围起来，等到他能够走动时，便护送③他进屋。动物们都不知道这是要干什么，只有本杰明除外，因为他心照不宣地点了点头，好像是明白了，不过，他缄口不言。

但是，数日过后，穆里尔自个儿念着那"七戒"条文时注意到，其中又有一条动物们都记错了。他们以为第五条戒律是"任何动物都不饮酒"，但他们忘记了其中的两个字。这条戒律真正是："任何动物都不饮酒过量。"

① brewing ['bru:iŋ] *n.* （酒的）酿造
② distilling [dis'tiliŋ] *n.* 蒸馏
③ escort ['eskɔ:t] *v.* 护送

Chapter IX

Boxer's split hoof was a long time in healing. They had started the rebuilding of the windmill the day after the victory celebrations were ended. Boxer refused to take even a day off work, and made it a point of honour not to let it be seen that he was in pain. In the evenings he would admit privately to Clover that the hoof troubled him a great deal. Clover treated the hoof with **poultices**① of herbs which she prepared by chewing them, and both she and Benjamin urged Boxer to work less hard. "A horse's lungs do not last for ever," she said to him. But Boxer would not listen. He had, he said, only one real ambition left—to see the windmill well under way before he reached the age for retirement.

At the beginning, when the laws of Animal Farm were first formulated, the retiring age had been fixed for horses and pigs at twelve, for cows at fourteen, for dogs at nine, for sheep at seven, and for hens and geese at five. **Liberal**② old-age pensions had been agreed upon. As yet no animal had actually retired on pension, but of late the subject had been discussed more and more. Now that the small field beyond the orchard had been set aside for barley, it was rumoured that a corner of the large pasture was to be fenced off and turned into a grazing-ground for **superannuated**③ animals. For a horse, it was said, the pension would be five pounds of corn a day and, in winter, fifteen pounds of hay, with a carrot or possibly an apple on public holidays. Boxer's twelfth birthday was due in the

第九章

拳击手那只开裂的蹄子很长时间都没有愈合。庆祝活动结束后的那一天，动物们便开始重建风车了。拳击手坚守劳动岗位，连一天都拒绝离开。他下定决心，绝对不让其他动物看出来，自己是忍着痛苦劳动的。到了晚上，他这才私下里对苜蓿说，蹄子疼得厉害。苜蓿把事先嚼烂的草药敷在他的蹄子上。她和本杰明都劝拳击手不要那么卖力干活儿。"马的肺部不可能永远经受得起折腾的。"她对他说。但是，拳击手就是不听。他说，他现在只有一个抱负——看到风车很好地运转，然后自己便退休。

刚开始，动物农场制定法律时，规定马和猪的退休年龄是十二岁，奶牛十五岁，狗九岁，绵羊七岁，母鸡和鹅五岁。已经做出了规定，要给退休动物发放足量的养老津贴。目前还没有任何动物领取养老津贴，但近来大家对这个问题的讨论越来越多起来。果园那边那片小牧场既然准备用来种植大麦，便有传言说，大牧场的一角准备围起来，用作年老动物的草场。据说，一匹马的养老津贴是一天五磅谷物，冬季里每天十五磅干草，节日期间还可以另加一根胡萝卜或者一个苹果。到了下一年的夏天，拳击手就十二岁了。

① poultice ['pəultis] *n.* 湿敷药物

② liberal ['libərəl] *a.* 充裕的

③ superannuated [ˌsjuːpərˈænjueitid] *a.* 退休的

· 141 ·

late summer of the following year.

Meanwhile life was hard. The winter was as cold as the last one had been, and food was even shorter. Once again all rations were reduced, except those of the pigs and the dogs. A too rigid equality in rations, Squealer explained, would have been contrary to the principles of Animalism. In any case he had no difficulty in proving to the other animals that they were not in reality short of food, whatever the appearances might be. For the time being, certainly, it had been found necessary to make a readjustment of rations (Squealer always spoke of it as a "readjustment," never as a "reduction"), but in comparison with the days of Jones, the improvement was enormous. Reading out the figures in a shrill, rapid voice, he proved to them in detail that they had more oats, more hay, more **turnips**① than they had had in Jones's day, that they worked shorter hours, that their drinking water was of better quality, that they lived longer, that a larger proportion of their young ones survived infancy, and that they had more straw in their stalls and suffered less from **fleas**②. The animals believed every word of it. Truth to tell, Jones and all he stood for had almost faded out of their memories. They knew that life nowadays was harsh and bare, that they were often hungry and often cold, and that they were usually working when they were not asleep. But doubtless it had been worse in the old days. They were glad to believe so. Besides, in those days they had been slaves and now they were free, and that made all the difference, as Squealer did not fail to point out.

There were many more mouths to feed now. In the autumn the four sows had all littered about simultaneously, producing thirty-one young pigs between them. The young pigs were **piebald**③, and as Napoleon was the only boar on the farm, it was possible to guess at their **parentage**④. It was announced that later, when bricks and timber had been purchased, a schoolroom would be built in the farmhouse garden. For the time being, the young pigs were given their instruction by Napoleon himself in the farmhouse kitchen. They took their exercise in the garden, and were discouraged from playing with the other young animals. About this time, too, it was laid down as a rule that when a pig and any

期间，动物们的生活很艰苦。冬天像头一年的冬天一样寒冷，而饲料更加匮乏。动物们的饲料配额再次削减，但猪和狗的配额除外。尖嗓子解释说，饲料配额上的绝对平等有悖"动物思想"的诸原则。任何情况下，尖嗓子都可轻而易举地向动物们证明，不管表面现象如何，他们实际上并不缺乏饲料。当然啦，就目前的情形而言，调整饲料配额是必要的（尖嗓子说到这件事情时总是用"调整"，而从来不用"削减"）。但是，同琼斯统治的时期比较起来，生活有了巨大的改善。他声音尖细，语速很快，大声念出了那些数字，详实地向动物们证明了，与琼斯统治的时期相比，他们拥有更多燕麦，更多干草料，更多胡萝卜。劳动的时间缩短了，饮用水质量更高了，他们的寿命延长了，幼崽的成活率提高了，窝棚里的干草更多了，侵扰他们的跳蚤更少了。动物们对尖嗓子所说的每一句都深信不疑。实话实说，琼斯和他所代表的一切几乎都从他们的记忆中淡出了。他们知道，眼下的生活很艰苦，饲料短缺。他们常常忍饥受冻。除了睡觉时间，他们一般都在干活儿。但是，毫无疑问，昔日里，情况更加糟糕。他们乐意相信这一点。此外，那些日子里，他们身为奴隶，但现在是自由的，这可是巨大的差别。尖嗓子会不失时机地指出这一点。

现在，动物农场需要供养的动物数目更多了。秋天里，四头母猪同时都下了幼崽，总共有三十一头小猪。小猪全是杂色的，由于拿破仑是农场上唯一的公猪，他们的身世便不言而喻了。已经宣布，以后，等买来了砖头和木料，拟在农场主住宅边的花园里盖一间教室。眼下，小猪们由拿破仑亲自施教，暂时安排在住宅的厨房里。他们在花园里做运动，不允许同别的小动物一块儿玩耍。大概也就在这段时间里，农场上已经定下了规矩，某一头猪若是在小路上同别的动

① turnip ['tə:nip] *n.* 萝卜

② flea [fli:] *n.* 跳蚤

③ piebald ['paibɔ:ld] *a.* 斑驳的
④ parentage ['pɛərəntidʒ] *n.* 出身

other animal met on the path, the other animal must stand aside: and also that all pigs, of whatever degree, were to have the privilege of wearing green ribbons on their tails on Sundays.

The farm had had a fairly successful year, but was still short of money. There were the bricks, sand, and lime for the schoolroom to be purchased, and it would also be necessary to begin saving up again for the machinery for the windmill. Then there were lamp oil and candles for the house, sugar for Napoleon's own table (he forbade this to the other pigs, on the ground that it made them fat), and all the usual replacements such as tools, nails, string, coal, wire, scrap-iron, and dog biscuits. A stump of hay and part of the potato crop were sold off, and the contract for eggs was increased to six hundred a week, so that that year the hens barely hatched enough chicks to keep their numbers at the same level. Rations, reduced in December, were reduced again in February, and lanterns in the stalls were forbidden to save Oil. But the pigs seemed comfortable enough, and in fact were putting on weight if anything. One afternoon in late February a warm, rich, appetising **scent**①, such as the animals had never smelt before, **wafted**② itself across the yard from the little brew-house, which had been disused in Jones's time, and which stood beyond the kitchen. Someone said it was the smell of cooking barley. The animals sniffed the air hungrily and wondered whether a warm mash was being prepared for their supper. But no warm mash appeared, and on the following Sunday it was announced that from now onwards all barley would be reserved for the pigs. The field beyond the orchard had already been sown with barley. And the news soon leaked out that every pig was now receiving a ration of a pint of beer daily, with half a gallon for Napoleon himself, which was always served to him in the Crown Derby soup **tureen**③.

But if there were hardships to be borne, they were partly **offset**④ by the fact that life nowadays had a greater dignity than it had had before. There were more songs, more speeches, more **processions**⑤. Napoleon had commanded that once a week there should be held something called a Spontaneous Demonstration, the object of which was to celebrate the struggles and triumphs of Animal Farm.

物相遇，另外的动物必须要靠边站。还有，所有猪，不管什么等级的，享有星期天在尾巴上系绿色饰带的特权。

农场这一年还算一帆风顺，但仍然资金短缺。盖一间教室需要购买砖头、沙子和石灰。为了购买将来风车需要的机械设备，他们还必须积累资金。此外，还需要室内照明用的煤油和蜡烛，以及拿破仑自己餐桌上所需的糖（他禁止别的猪食用糖，因为食用糖会发胖）。还需要不断添补各种易耗物品，诸如工具、钉子、绳索、煤炭、铁丝、铁块，以及狗食用的饼干。他们卖掉了一堆干草料和一部分收获的土豆。售蛋合同已经增加到了每星期六百枚，所以当年母鸡孵出的小鸡的数量几乎都难以维持原有的水平。十二月份已经削减的饲料配额到了二月份再次削减了。为了节省煤油，动物的窝棚禁止掌灯。但是，那些猪似乎过得够舒心惬意的。事实上，不说别的，他们体重就增加了。二月下旬的一天下午，动物们闻到了一股从未闻过的香气，温暖浓郁，鲜美开胃。香味是从院落一边的小酿酒房飘溢出来的。酿酒房在琼斯时代已经弃用，坐落在厨房的后面。有动物说，这是蒸煮大麦的气味。动物们如饥似渴地吸着香气，心里思忖着，说不定他们晚餐可以吃上热乎乎的大麦糊呢。但是，他们并没有见到大麦糊的影子。随后的那个星期天，动物们接到通知，从今往后，全部大麦都将留给猪食用。果园那边的那片田地已经种植了大麦。而很快又有消息传出，每头猪每天可以得到一品脱啤酒的配额，拿破仑自己则享用半个加仑，啤酒是盛在王冠德比的汤碗里给他享用的。

虽说他们现在还要忍受种种艰难困苦，但是，他们比过去生活得更加有尊严。这个事实在一定程度上消解了他们面临的困境。歌声更多、演讲更多、游行更多。拿破仑已经下达了命令，每个星期都要举行名为"自发式游行"的活动，旨在庆祝动物农场的斗争

① scent [sent] *n.* 味道
② waft [wɔft] *v.* 使飘荡

③ tureen [təˈriːn] *n.* 盖碗
④ offset [ˈɔfˈset] *v.* 抵消

⑤ procession [prəuˈseʃən] *n.* 队伍

At the appointed time the animals would leave their work and march round the **precincts**① of the farm in military formation, with the pigs leading, then the horses, then the cows, then the sheep, and then the poultry. The dogs **flanked**② the procession and at the head of all marched Napoleon's black cockerel. Boxer and Clover always carried between them a green banner marked with the hoof and the horn and the **caption**③, "Long live Comrade Napoleon!" Afterwards there were recitations of poems composed in Napoleon's honour, and a speech by Squealer giving particulars of the latest increases in the production of foodstuffs, and on occasion a shot was fired from the gun. The sheep were the greatest **devotees**④ of the Spontaneous Demonstration, and if anyone complained (as a few animals sometimes did, when no pigs or dogs were near) that they wasted time and meant a lot of standing about in the cold, the sheep were sure to silence him with a tremendous bleating of "Four legs good, two legs bad!" But by and large the animals enjoyed these celebrations. They found it comforting to be reminded that, after all, they were truly their own masters and that the work they did was for their own benefit. So that, what with the songs, the processions, Squealer's lists of figures, the thunder of the gun, the **crowing**⑤ of the cockerel, and the fluttering of the flag, they were able to forget that their bellies were empty, at least part of the time.

In April, Animal Farm was proclaimed a Republic, and it became necessary to elect a President. There was only one candidate, Napoleon, who was elected unanimously. On the same day it was given out that fresh documents had been discovered which revealed further details about Snowball's **complicity**⑥ with Jones. It now appeared that Snowball had not, as the animals had previously imagined, merely attempted to lose the Battle of the Cowshed by means of a **stratagem**⑦, but had been openly fighting on Jones's side. In fact, it was he who had actually been the leader of the human forces, and had charged into battle with the words "Long live Humanity!" on his lips. The wounds on Snowball's back, which a few of the animals still remembered to have seen, had been **inflicted**⑧ by Napoleon's teeth.

① precinct ['pri:siŋkt] *n.* 管辖
区
② flank [flæŋk] *v.* 位于……
的侧面

③ caption ['kæpʃən] *n.* 说明
文字

④ devotee [,devə'ti:] *n.* 献身
者

⑤ crowing [krəuiŋ] *n.* 啼叫

⑥ complicity [kəm'plisəti] *n.*
同谋关系

⑦ stratagem ['strætədʒəm] *n.*
诡计，阴谋

⑧ inflict [in'flikt] *v.* 施予

和胜利。到了规定的时间，动物们就会离开工作岗位，排着军旅的队伍在农场的地界内绕行，猪走在队伍前列，第二是马，紧接着是奶牛，随后是绵羊，最后是禽类。狗行进在队伍的两侧，而位于队伍之首的是拿破仑那只黑色小公鸡。拳击手和苜蓿二位同时扛着那面绘着兽蹄和兽角的绿色旗帜，旗帜上还有"拿破仑同志万岁"的字样。游行过后，还要朗诵专门歌颂拿破仑的诗歌。尖嗓子还要发表演说，报告最近粮食生产增加的具体数据。有时候，还要鸣枪。绵羊是"自发式游行"中最投入的。如果有哪个动物抱怨说（一旦附近没有猪或者狗，少数动物就会如此），他们这是浪费时间，大家还要在寒冷的天气里长时间站立，绵羊们肯定就会咩咩地念叨起"四条腿好，两条腿坏！"，令那只抱怨的动物闭嘴不说。但是，总体上来看，动物们还是很喜欢这类庆祝活动的。他们发现，通过这些活动，他们很欣慰地意识到，自己是真正的主人了，他们干活儿是为了自己的利益。因此，阵阵歌声，支支游行队伍，尖嗓子列举的串串数据，枪声巨响，公鸡鸣叫，旗帜招展，通过这一切，动物们能够忘却他们正饥肠辘辘，至少部分时间里如此。

四月里，动物农场宣布成立"共和国"，因此，有必要选举总统。只有一位候选人，即拿破仑。他被大家一致选为总统。同一天，据报道，动物农场发现了新的文件，其中透露出雪球同琼斯勾结的更多细节。现在看起来，情况并非如动物们先前想象的那样，雪球仅仅是企图通过玩弄阴谋手段导致"牛棚之战"失败，而是公开为琼斯而战。事实上，他亲临战场，指挥人类武力进犯。他嘴里喊着"人类万岁"的口号，冲锋陷阵。少数动物仍然记得，他们看见雪球背上负伤了，而那些伤痕实际上是拿破仑的牙齿咬破的。

In the middle of the summer Moses the raven suddenly reappeared on the farm, after an absence of several years. He was quite unchanged, still did no work, and talked in the same **strain**① as ever about Sugarcandy Mountain. He would perch on a stump, **flap**② his black wings, and talk by the hour to anyone who would listen. "Up there, comrades," he would say solemnly, pointing to the sky with his large beak—"up there, just on the other side of that dark cloud that you can see there it lies, Sugarcandy Mountain, that happy country where we poor animals shall rest for ever from our labours!" He even claimed to have been there on one of his higher flights, and to have seen the everlasting fields of clover and the linseed cake and lump sugar growing on the hedges. Many of the animals believed him. Their lives now, they reasoned, were hungry and laborious; was it not right and just that a better world should exist somewhere else? A thing that was difficult to determine was the attitude of the pigs towards Moses. They all declared contemptuously that his stories about Sugarcandy Mountain were lies, and yet they allowed him to remain on the farm, not working, with an allowance of a **gill**③ of beer a day.

After his hoof had healed up, Boxer worked harder than ever. Indeed, all the animals worked like slaves that year. Apart from the regular work of the farm, and the rebuilding of the windmill, there was the schoolhouse for the young pigs, which was started in March. Sometimes the long hours on insufficient food were hard to bear, but Boxer never **faltered**④. In nothing that he said or did was there any sign that his strength was not what it had been. It was only his appearance that was a little altered; his **hide**⑤ was less shiny than it had used to be, and his great **haunches**⑥ seemed to have shrunken. The others said, "Boxer will pick up when the spring grass comes on"; but the spring came and Boxer grew no fatter. Sometimes on the slope leading to the top of the quarry, when he **braced**⑦ his muscles against the weight of some vast boulder, it seemed that nothing kept him on his feet except the will to continue. At such times his lips were seen to form the words, "I will work harder"; he had no voice left. Once again Clover and Benjamin warned him to take care of his health, but Boxer

① strain [strein] *n.* 口吻
② flap [flæp] *v.* 拍打

仲夏时分，渡鸦摩西失踪了几年之后突然出现在了农场。他没有什么变化，还是什么活儿都不干。一如既往地唱着关于"糖果山"的老调儿。他会栖息在一个树桩上，拍打着自己黑色的翅膀，但凡有哪只动物愿意听，他会说上一个小时。"在那儿啊，同志们，"他会说，语气郑重其事，一边用自己的大嘴指着天空——"在那儿，就在你们看得见的那团乌云的另一边，糖果山就在那儿呢。那是个幸福美满的国度，可怜的动物们不需要劳动，便可以永远歇息！"他甚至声称，自己有一次飞得很高，都已经飞到那儿了，看见了那儿四季常青的苜蓿，树篱上结出了亚麻籽饼干和糖块。许多动物都相信他的说法。他们分析着，自己现在的生活食不果腹，辛苦劳累。现如今，有个更加理想的地方存在于世界的某处，这难道不是很正常的事情吗？难以捉摸的是那些猪对待摩西是什么态度。他们全都不屑一顾地声称，摩西关于"糖果山"的故事完全子虚乌有。不过，他们还是允许他待在农场，不干活儿，每天可以享受七分之一升啤酒的津贴。

③ gill [gil] *n.* 吉耳（液量单位）

拳击手的蹄子愈合了之后，干活儿比过去更加卖力了。确实，当年，所有动物都像奴隶一样干着活儿。农场上的常规活儿要干，还要干风车重建的活儿，除此之外，还要替小猪们盖那间教室，工程从三月份就动工了。有时候，长时间填不饱肚子，令动物们难以忍受。但是，拳击手的脚步从来都不打颤。从他的言谈举止中，看不出任何体力不如从前的迹象。他只是音容相貌上略微有

④ falter ['fɔ:ltə] *v.* 蹒跚，踉跄

⑤ hide [haid] *n.* 兽皮
⑥ haunch [hɔ:ntʃ] *n.* 胯部

点变化而已，皮毛不如过去有光泽，壮实敦厚的后胯似乎萎缩松弛了一点儿。其他动物说"等到春天来了，牧草嫩绿了，拳击手定会恢复先前的容貌"。但是，春天来了，拳击手并没有长膘。有时，他绷紧着肌肉，拖着沉重的巨石，顺着采石场的斜坡向顶端拖行，这时候，支撑着他的脚步继续前行的除了意志力仿佛没有别的什么了。每当这种时候，动物们便看到他嘴唇嗫嚅着，似

⑦ brace [breis] *v.* 使绷紧

paid no attention. His twelfth birthday was approaching. He did not care what happened so long as a good store of stone was accumulated before he went on pension.

Late one evening in the summer, a sudden rumour ran round the farm that something had happened to Boxer. He had gone out alone to drag a load of stone down to the windmill. And sure enough, the rumour was true. A few minutes later two pigeons came racing in with the news: "Boxer has fallen! He is lying on his side and can't get up!"

About half the animals on the farm rushed out to the knoll where the windmill stood. There lay Boxer, between the shafts of the cart, his neck stretched out, unable even to raise his head. His eyes were **glazed**[①], his sides **matted**[②] with sweat. A thin stream of blood had trickled out of his mouth. Clover dropped to her knees at his side.

"Boxer!" she cried, "how are you?"

"It is my lung," said Boxer in a weak voice. "It does not matter. I think you will be able to finish the windmill without me. There is a pretty good store of stone accumulated. I had only another month to go in any case. To tell you the truth, I had been looking forward to my retirement. And perhaps, as Benjamin is growing old too, they will let him retire at the same time and be a companion to me."

"We must get help at once," said Clover. "Run, somebody, and tell Squealer what has happened."

All the other animals immediately raced back to the farmhouse to give Squealer the news. Only Clover remained, and Benjamin who lay down at Boxer's side, and, without speaking, kept the flies off him with his long tail. After about a quarter of an hour Squealer appeared, full of sympathy and concern. He said that Comrade Napoleon had learned with the very deepest distress of this misfortune to one of the most loyal workers on the farm, and was already making arrangements to send Boxer to be treated in the hospital at Willingdon. The animals felt a little uneasy at this. Except for Mollie and Snowball, no other animal had ever left the farm, and they did not like to think of their sick

乎在说"我要更加卖力干活儿"。他无法用声音说出来。苜蓿和本杰明再次提醒他要注意自己的身体，但拳击手毫不理会。他的十二岁生日临近了。只要能够在自己领取养老津贴之前凑齐足够石料，其余的事情他都不放在心上。

夏天的一个晚上，时间不早了，农场上突然出现传言，说拳击手出事了。他独自外出拖一车石料到风车工地。很显然，传言属实。几分钟过后，两只鸽子急速飞了回来，带回来这样的消息："拳击手倒下了！他身子侧躺在地上，爬不起来了！"

农场大概有一半动物冲到风车所在的小山丘。拳击手躺在那儿，身子处于大车的两辕之间，脖子前伸着，连头都抬不起来了。他两眼目光呆滞，身子的两侧汗津津的。鲜血从嘴里流了出来，形成了一道小的血流。苜蓿跪在他身旁。

"拳击手！"她大声呼喊着，"你这是怎么啦？"

"是我肺部的问题，"拳击手说着，声音很微弱，"没有关系的。我相信，离开了我，你们能够完成风车工程。石料已经凑得够多了。无论怎么说，我也就只有一个月时间干活儿了。实话告诉你吧，我一直盼望着退休呢。说不定啊，因为本杰明年岁已高，他们会让他同一时间退休，可以和我做伴来着。"

"我们必须得立刻叫其他动物来帮忙，"苜蓿说，"哪一位，快跑啊，去把发生的情况告诉尖嗓子。"

所有其他动物立刻跑回农场主住宅，把情况告诉给尖嗓子。只留下了苜蓿，还有本杰明——在拳击手身边躺下，一声不吭，用自己的长尾巴驱赶苍蝇。大概一刻钟过后，尖嗓子到达了现场，充满了同情和忧虑。他说，拿破仑得知农场上最忠诚的劳动者之一发生了如此不幸，痛惜不已。他正在着手做出安排，拟送拳击手前往威灵登的医院接受治疗。对此，动物们感到有点不安。除了莫莉和雪球之外，任何其他动物都不曾离开过

① glaze [gleiz] v. 变呆滞

② matte [mæt] v. 使……无光

comrade in the hands of human beings. However, Squealer easily convinced them that the **veterinary**① **surgeon**② in Willingdon could treat Boxer's case more satisfactorily than could be done on the farm. And about half an hour later, when Boxer had somewhat recovered, he was with difficulty got on to his feet, and managed to limp back to his stall, where Clover and Benjamin had prepared a good bed of straw for him.

For the next two days Boxer remained in his stall. The pigs had sent out a large bottle of pink medicine which they had found in the medicine **chest**③ in the bathroom, and Clover administered it to Boxer twice a day after meals. In the evenings she lay in his stall and talked to him, while Benjamin kept the flies off him. Boxer professed not to be sorry for what had happened. If he made a good recovery, he might expect to live another three years, and he looked forward to the peaceful days that he would spend in the corner of the big pasture. It would be the first time that he had had leisure to study and improve his mind. He intended, he said, to devote the rest of his life to learning the remaining twenty-two letters of the alphabet.

However, Benjamin and Clover could only be with Boxer after working hours, and it was in the middle of the day when the van came to take him away. The animals were all at work weeding turnips under the supervision of a pig, when they were astonished to see Benjamin come galloping from the direction of the farm buildings, **braying**④ at the top of his voice. It was the first time that they had ever seen Benjamin excite — indeed, it was the first time that anyone had ever seen him gallop. "Quick, quick!" he shouted. "Come at once! They're taking Boxer away!" Without waiting for orders from the pig, the animals broke off work and raced back to the farm buildings. Sure enough, there in the yard was a large closed van, drawn by two horses, with lettering on its side and a sly-looking man in a low-crowned **bowler**⑤ hat sitting on the driver's seat. And Boxer's stall was empty.

The animals crowded round the van. "Good-bye, Boxer!" they **chorused**⑥, "good-bye!"

① veterinary ['vetərinəri] *n.* 兽医的

② surgeon ['səːdʒən] *n.* 外科医生

③ chest [tʃest] *n.* 箱子

④ bray [brei] *v.*（驴）叫

⑤ bowler hat 圆顶高帽

⑥ chorus ['kɔːrəs] *v.* 齐声

农场。他们不愿意想象，把自己生病的同志交到人类的手上去。不过，尖嗓子轻而易举便让他们相信了，威灵登的兽医能够医治拳击手的疾病，治疗的效果比待在农场上更加理想。大概半个小时之后，拳击手的病情稍有好转，他好不容易挣扎着站立了起来，一瘸一拐地走回到了自己的厩棚，苜蓿和本杰明在那儿替他准备好了舒适的干草床铺。

随后的两天中，拳击手待在自己的厩棚里。猪送来了一大瓶他们在浴室的药柜里找到的药。苜蓿每天都让拳击手饭后服两次药。到了晚上，她就躺在他的厩棚里，同他说话交谈，本杰明则给他驱赶苍蝇。拳击手坦言说，自己对已经发生的事情并不后悔。他若是身体恢复得好，还有望再活三年呢。他期待着那平静安宁的日子，到时可以在大牧场的一角安度晚年。那将是他一生中头一次有闲暇学习，改善心智。他说，他打算全心全意，用自己的余生来学会剩下的那二十二个字母[1]。

然而，本杰明和苜蓿只能在干活之余来陪伴拳击手。那是在中午时分，一辆大车把他给接走了。当时，动物们在一头猪的监督下给萝卜地除草，突然，他们很惊讶地看到，本杰明从农场窝棚的方向飞奔过来，一边声嘶力竭地大喊着。动物们这是头一回看见本杰明情绪激动。这也是头一回有动物看见他急速奔跑。"快！快呀！"他大声喊着，"立刻过去！他们正把拳击手送走呢！"不等猪下达命令，动物们立刻放下手上的活儿，急忙跑回农场的窝棚区。果不其然，院落里停着一辆密封的运货大车，有两匹马拉着，大车侧身写着字，驾车座上坐着一位相貌诡秘的男子，只见他头上戴着低顶圆礼帽。拳击手的厩棚里是空的。

动物们把大车团团围住。"再见啦，拳击手！"他们齐声呼喊，"再见啦！"

---

1 前面已有描述，拳击手好不容易才学会了开头的四个字母。

"Fools! Fools!" shouted Benjamin, **prancing**① round them and stamping the earth with his small hoofs. "Fools! Do you not see what is written on the side of that van?"

That gave the animals pause, and there was a **hush**②. Muriel began to spell out the words. But Benjamin pushed her aside and in the midst of a deadly silence he read:

" 'Alfred Simmonds, Horse Slaughterer and Glue Boiler, Willingdon. Dealer in Hides and Bone-Meal. Kennels Supplied.' Do you not understand what that means? They are taking Boxer to the knacker's!"

A cry of horror burst from all the animals. At this moment the man on the box whipped up his horses and the van moved out of the yard at a smart trot. All the animals followed, crying out at the tops of their voices. Clover forced her way to the front. The van began to gather speed. Clover tried to stir her stout limbs to a gallop, and achieved a **canter**③. "Boxer!" she cried. "Boxer! Boxer! Boxer!" And just at this moment, as though he had heard the uproar outside, Boxer's face, with the white stripe down his nose, appeared at the small window at the back of the van.

"Boxer!" cried Clover in a terrible voice. "Boxer! Get out! Get out quickly! They're taking you to your death!"

All the animals took up the cry of "Get out, Boxer, get out!" But the van was already gathering speed and drawing away from them. It was uncertain whether Boxer had understood what Clover had said. But a moment later his face disappeared from the window and there was the sound of a tremendous drumming of hoofs inside the van. He was trying to kick his way out. The time had been when a few kicks from Boxer's hoofs would have smashed the van to matchwood. But alas! his strength had left him; and in a few moments the sound of drumming hoofs grew fainter and died away. In desperation the animals began appealing to the two horses which drew the van to stop. "Comrades, comrades!" they shouted. "Don't take your own brother to his death! " But the stupid **brutes**④, too ignorant to realise what was happening, merely set back

① prance [prɑ:ns] v. 后足立地腾跃

② hush [hʌʃ] n. 变得寂静

③ canter ['kæntə] n.（马的）慢跑

④ brute [bru:t] n. 畜生

"傻瓜！傻瓜！"本杰明大声吼着，一边在他们周围腾起身子，小蹄子踢着地上的泥土，"傻瓜！你们难道没有看见大车侧身上写着什么字吗？"

动物们听到这么一说愣住了，安静了下来。穆里尔开始拼读出车身上那些字。但是，本杰明把她推到了一旁。一片寂静之中，他念出了声来：

"'阿尔弗雷德·西蒙兹，威灵登马匹屠宰商兼熬胶商。经营兽皮和骨粉，同时供应狗舍。'你们难道不知道这是什么意思吗？他们这是要把拳击手送到屠宰场去啊！"

动物们顿时发出了恐怖的尖叫声。这个当儿，驾车的男子朝着他的马一挥鞭子，马一路小跑着把车拉出了院落。所有动物都跟在大车后面，扯起嗓子高声大喊着。苜蓿挤到了最前头。大车开始加速了。苜蓿竭尽全力，抬起四条腿狂奔了起来，但只达到了马匹慢跑的速度。"拳击手！"她大声喊着，"拳击手！拳击手！拳击手！"就在这一刻，拳击手似乎听见了车外的呼喊声，便把脸伸出大车后面的小窗户，露出了鼻梁上那一道白毛。

"拳击手！"苜蓿大喊着，叫喊声很恐怖，"拳击手！出来呀！赶快出来呀！他们把你送走是要你的命啊！"

所有动物也都跟着大喊起来，"出来呀，拳击手，出来呀！"但是，大车已经加速了，驶离了他们。不知道拳击手是否明白了苜蓿说的话。但是，片刻之后，他的脸从窗口消失了，车内传来如击鼓般蹄子蹬踢的巨响。他拼命地想要从大车里挣脱出来。若是在过去，拳击手只消几蹄子便会把大车像个火柴盒似的踢个稀巴烂。但是，现在不行啊！他已经没有体力了。一会儿过后，击鼓似的蹄子蹬踢声越来越微弱，最后消失了。绝望之中，动物们开始恳求拉车的两匹马停下来。"同志们，同志们啊！"他们大声喊着，"别拉着你们的同志去送死啊！"但是，两匹愚笨的马太过愚昧无知了，根

their ears and quickened their pace. Boxer's face did not reappear at the window. Too late, someone thought of racing ahead and shutting the five-barred gate; but in another moment the van was through it and rapidly disappearing down the road. Boxer was never seen again.

Three days later it was announced that he had died in the hospital at Willingdon, in spite of receiving every attention a horse could have. Squealer came to announce the news to the others. He had, he said, been present during Boxer's last hours.

"It was the most affecting sight I have ever seen!" said Squealer, lifting his trotter and wiping away a tear. "I was at his bedside at the very last. And at the end, almost too weak to speak, he whispered in my ear that his sole sorrow was to have passed on before the windmill was finished. 'Forward, comrades!' he whispered. 'Forward in the name of the Rebellion. Long live Animal Farm! Long live Comrade Napoleon! Napoleon is always right.' Those were his very last words, comrades."

Here Squealer's **demeanour**① suddenly changed. He fell silent for a moment, and his little eyes **darted**② suspicious glances from side to side before he proceeded.

It had come to his knowledge, he said, that a foolish and **wicked**③ rumour had been circulated at the time of Boxer's removal. Some of the animals had noticed that the van which took Boxer away was marked "Horse Slaughterer," and had actually jumped to the conclusion that Boxer was being sent to the knacker's. It was almost unbelievable, said Squealer, that any animal could be so stupid. Surely, he cried indignantly, whisking his tail and skipping from side to side, surely they knew their beloved Leader, Comrade Napoleon, better than that? But the explanation was really very simple. The van had previously been the property of the knacker, and had been bought by the veterinary surgeon, who had not yet painted the old name out. That was how the mistake had arisen.

The animals were enormously relieved to hear this. And when Squealer went on to give further **graphic**④ details of Boxer's death-bed, the admirable

本搞不懂正在发生的事情，只顾着竖起耳朵，加速前行。拳击手的脸没有再在窗户口出现了。为时已晚，某只动物想到要冲上前去，关上五道闩的大门。但是，又过了一会儿，大车通过了大门口，急速地消失在大路尽头。动物们从此再也没有见过拳击手。

三天过后，农场上宣布了，拳击手尽管得到了马匹能够享受到的精心照料，但还是在威灵登的医院里去世了。尖嗓子对其他动物通报了这个消息。他说，拳击手处在弥留之际时，他一直在场。

"那可是我所经历的最最感动的场景啊！"尖嗓子说，一边抬起一个蹄子抹掉眼泪，"最后时刻，我守在他的病床边。最后，他过于虚弱，说不出话来了，便对我耳语说，他唯一感到悲伤的就是未能看到风车工程竣工。'前进吧，同志们！'他低声说着，'以反抗运动的名义，前进吧！动物农场万岁！拿破仑同志万岁！拿破仑总是对的。'以上就是他最后说的话，同志们啊。"

说到这儿，尖嗓子的态度陡然发生了变化。他沉默了片刻，小眼睛左右扫视了一番，充满了迟疑，然后继续说话。

他说，根据他的了解，拳击手被送走时，出现了愚蠢而又邪恶的谣言，说有的动物注意到了，把拳击手送走的大车上写有"马匹屠宰商"的字样，并且草率地得出结论说，拳击手被送到屠宰场去了。尖嗓子说，简直令人无法置信的是，竟然有动物愚不可及到如此地步。毫无疑问，他大声训斥着，义愤填膺，尾巴摇晃着，身子左蹦右跳着。想必他们对我们敬爱的领袖拿破仑的了解不止于此吧？但是，解释其实非常简单。运货车先前是属于屠宰商的财产，后来兽医给买过来了，后者没有把先前的名字给涂掉。这样便引起了误解。

听了这一番解释后，动物们大大地松了一口气。然后，尖嗓子继续绘声绘色地描述拳击手临终时的细节，

① demeanour [di'mi:nə] *n.* 态度
② dart [dɑːt] *v.* 投射
③ wicked ['wikid] *a.* 邪恶的
④ graphic ['græfik] *a.* 生动的

care he had received, and the expensive medicines for which Napoleon had paid without a thought as to the cost, their last doubts disappeared and the sorrow that they felt for their comrade's death was **tempered**① by the thought that at least he had died happy.

Napoleon himself appeared at the meeting on the following Sunday morning and pronounced a short **oration**② in Boxer's honour. It had not been possible, he said, to bring back their lamented comrade's remains for **interment**③ on the farm, but he had ordered a large **wreath**④ to be made from the **laurels**⑤ in the farmhouse garden and sent down to be placed on Boxer's grave. And in a few days' time the pigs intended to hold a memorial **banquet**⑥ in Boxer's honour. Napoleon ended his speech with a reminder of Boxer's two favourite maxims, "I will work harder" and "Comrade Napoleon is always right", maxims, he said, which every animal would do well to adopt as his own.

On the day appointed for the banquet, a grocer's van drove up from Willingdon and delivered a large wooden **crate**⑦ at the farmhouse. That night there was the sound of **uproarious**⑧ singing, which was followed by what sounded like a violent quarrel and ended at about eleven o'clock with a tremendous crash of glass. No one stirred in the farmhouse before noon on the following day, and the word went round that from somewhere or other the pigs had acquired the money to buy themselves another case of whisky.

他如何受到无微不至的照料，拿破仑如何不惜一切代价，支付巨额医药费。这时候，动物们的疑惑烟消云散了。他们虽然因自己的同志不幸离世感到悲痛，但是，一想到他至少死得很安详，便得到了些许安慰。

随后那个星期天的上午，拿破仑亲自出席会议。他为悼念拳击手发表了一段简短的演说。虽然无法将自己已经亡故的同志的遗体运回来安葬在农场，但是，已经吩咐过了，要用农场花园的月桂树枝编织一个大花环，送去放置在拳击手的墓旁。猪还打算几天后举行一次追思性的宴会。拿破仑最后引述了拳击手常常挂在嘴边的那两句座右铭："我要更加卖力干活儿"和"拿破仑同志总是对的"。他说，每只动物都要把这些座右铭当成自己的座右铭。

到了预定举行宴会的那天，有一辆杂货商的运货车从威灵顿驶来，把一个大木箱卸在农场主住宅边。当晚，住宅里传来了嘹亮的歌声，紧接着听上去像是愤怒的争吵声。最后，大概十一点钟的样子，随着打碎玻璃杯子的声音，喧闹声结束了。翌日，中午之前，整个宅邸里毫无半点动静。有传言说，那些猪不知从什么地方弄到了钱，替自己又买了一箱威士忌酒。

① temper ['tempə] v. 缓和

② oration [ɔː'reiʃən] n. 演说
③ interment [in'təːmənt] n. 安葬
④ wreath [riːθ] n. 花环
⑤ laurel ['lɔrəl] n. 月桂
⑥ banquet ['bæŋkwit] n. 盛宴，筵席

⑦ crate [kreit] n. 板条箱
⑧ uproarious [ʌp'rɔːriəs] a. 吵闹的

Chapter X

Years passed. The seasons came and went, the short animal lives fled by. A time came when there was no one who remembered the old days before the Rebellion, except Clover, Benjamin, Moses the raven, and a number of the pigs.

Muriel was dead; Bluebell, Jessie, and Pincher were dead. Jones too was dead—he had died in an **inebriates**[①]' home in another part of the country. Snowball was forgotten. Boxer was forgotten, except by the few who had known him. Clover was an old stout mare now, stiff in the **joints**[②] and with a tendency to **rheumy**[③] eyes. She was two years past the retiring age, but in fact no animal had ever actually retired. The talk of setting aside a corner of the pasture for superannuated animals had long since been dropped. Napoleon was now a mature boar of twenty-four stone. Squealer was so fat that he could with difficulty see out of his eyes. Only old Benjamin was much the same as ever, except for being a little greyer about the muzzle, and, since Boxer's death, more **morose**[④] and **taciturn**[⑤] than ever.

There were many more creatures on the farm now, though the increase was not so great as had been expected in earlier years. Many animals had been born to whom the Rebellion was only a **dim**[⑥] tradition, passed on by word of mouth, and others had been bought who had never heard mention of such a thing before their arrival. The farm possessed three horses now besides Clover.

第十章

① inebriate [i'ni:briət] *n.* 酗酒之徒

② joint [dʒɔint] *n.* 关节
③ rheumy ['ru:mi] *a.* 黏湿的

④ morose [mə'rəus] *a.* 忧郁的
⑤ taciturn ['tæsitə:n] *a.* 沉默寡言的
⑥ dim [dim] *a.* 昏暗的

岁月流逝，寒来暑往。寿命较短的动物都相继死去了。终于有那么一天，除了苜蓿、本杰明、渡鸦摩西和一些猪之外，没有任何动物记得反抗运动爆发之前那些旧日的光景了。

穆里尔去世了。蓝铃、杰西和平彻去世了。琼斯也已经去世了——他是在本郡另外一处地方的酗酒者收容所内离世的。雪球被遗忘了。拳击手也被遗忘了，只有极少数熟悉他的动物记得起他。苜蓿已经进入耄耋之年，体形肥胖，关节僵硬，双眼总是充满了黏液。她到达退休年龄已经两年了，但是，事实上，没有任何动物真正退休过。大牧场的一角预留给高龄动物使用的说法已经很长时间没有谈起了。拿破仑现在已经长成为一头三百多磅重的大公猪了。尖嗓子也很肥胖，眼睛看东西都十分费劲。只有本杰明还和过去一样没有什么变化，只是面部的毛略微灰白了一些。而且，自从拳击手去世之后，他更加闷闷不乐，沉默寡言。

现在，农场的动物数量增加了许多，不过，增加的幅度不如早些年预期的那么大。许多动物在农场出生，但对他们而言，反抗运动只是个模糊的传说而已，那也是从动物们的口口相传当中听来的。另外一些动物则是从别处买来的，他们到达此地之前从未听到有

They were fine upstanding beasts, willing workers and good comrades, but very stupid. None of them proved able to learn the alphabet beyond the letter B. They accepted everything that they were told about the Rebellion and the principles of Animalism, especially from Clover, for whom they had an almost **filial**[①] respect; but it was doubtful whether they understood very much of it. The farm was more prosperous now, and better organised: it had even been enlarged by two fields which had been bought from Mr. Pilkington. The windmill had been successfully completed at last, and the farm possessed a threshing machine and a hay elevator of its own, and various new buildings had been added to it. Whymper had bought himself a dogcart. The windmill, however, had not after all been used for generating electrical power. It was used for milling corn, and brought in a handsome money profit. The animals were hard at work building yet another windmill; when that one was finished, so it was said, the dynamos would be installed. But the luxuries of which Snowball had once taught the animals to dream, the stalls with electric light and hot and cold water, and the three-day week, were no longer talked about. Napoleon had **denounced**[②] such ideas as contrary to the spirit of Animalism. The truest happiness, he said, lay in working hard and living frugally.

Somehow it seemed as though the farm had grown richer without making the animals themselves any richer, except, of course, for the pigs and the dogs. Perhaps this was partly because there were so many pigs and so many dogs. It was not that these creatures did not work, after their fashion. There was, as Squealer was never tired of explaining, endless work in the supervision and organisation of the farm. Much of this work was of a kind that the other animals were too ignorant to understand. For example, Squealer told them that the pigs had to **expend**[③] enormous labours every day upon mysterious things called "files," "reports," "**minutes**[④]," and "**memoranda**[⑤]." These were large sheets of paper which had to be closely covered with writing, and as soon as they were so covered, they were burnt in the **furnace**[⑥]. This was of the highest importance for the welfare of the farm, Squealer said. But still, neither pigs nor dogs produced

① filial ['filjəl] *a.* 孝顺的

② denounce [di'nauns] *v.* 指责

③ expend [ik'spend] *v.* 花费
④ minute ['minit] *n.* 会议记录
⑤ memoranda [ˌmemə'rændə] *n.* 备忘录（memorandum 的复数）
⑥ furnace ['fə:nis] *n.* 炉子

动物提及这样的事情。除了苜蓿之外，农场现在还有三匹马，全是体格健壮的牲口，勤奋干活儿，是些好同志，但就是十分愚笨。他们认识的字母仅限于头两个，后面的都不认识。关于反抗运动的情况和动物思想原则，怎么对他们说，他们都一股脑儿地接受。尤其是苜蓿说的，他们对她近乎孝顺，毕恭毕敬。不过，苜蓿说的话，他们是否听明白了，那倒是值得怀疑。现在，农场景象更加繁荣，组织更加有序。农场的面积扩大了，因为他们从皮尔金顿手上买来了两片田地。风车终于建造完成了。农场上有了一台打谷机，一台干草码垛机，还新近盖起了各种窝棚。温佩尔给自己购买了一辆轻便马车。不过，风车没有用来发电，而是用来碾磨谷物，这样倒是带来了可观的金钱收入。动物们卖力干活儿，还要再建造一座风车。据说，等到新的风车竣工之后，他们拟安装发电机组。不过，雪球曾经教导动物们憧憬的奢华生活情景——窝棚里有电灯，有冷热水，每星期工作三天——现在再也不谈了。拿破仑谴责这样的理念有悖动物思想的精神。他说，最真实的幸福生活在于努力工作，生活简朴。

不知怎么回事，农场虽然看起来更加富裕了，但动物们自己感觉不到富裕，当然，猪和狗除外。或许部分原因是，猪和狗的数量过多。这倒并不是说这些动物没有按照自己的方式劳动。正如尖嗓子不知疲倦地解释过的那样，农场上的监管和组织工作没完没了。这一类的工作由于其他动物愚昧无知，无法理解，大部分都无法胜任。比如，尖嗓子告诉他们说，猪每天都要把大量的劳动耗费在所谓"档案""报告""会议记录"和"备忘录"等等神秘的事务上。那些都是很大的纸张，上面密密麻麻地写满了文字。而等到写满了之后，便又扔进火炉付之一炬了。为了农场的福祉，这一切至关重要，尖嗓子如是说。不过，话说回来，猪和狗并不凭着自身的劳动生产粮食。而他们的数量

any food by their own labour; and there were very many of them, and their appetites were always good.

As for the others, their life, so far as they knew, was as it had always been. They were generally hungry, they slept on straw, they drank from the pool, they laboured in the fields; in winter they were troubled by the cold, and in summer by the flies. Sometimes the older ones among them **racked**① their dim memories and tried to determine whether in the early days of the Rebellion, when Jones's expulsion was still recent, things had been better or worse than now. They could not remember. There was nothing with which they could compare their present lives: they had nothing to go upon except Squealer's lists of figures, which **invariably**② demonstrated that everything was getting better and better. The animals found the problem insoluble; in any case, they had little time for speculating on such things now. Only old Benjamin professed to remember every detail of his long life and to know that things never had been, nor ever could be much better or much worse—hunger, hardship, and disappointment being, so he said, the unalterable law of life.

And yet the animals never gave up hope. More, they never lost, even for an instant, their sense of honour and privilege in being members of Animal Farm. They were still the only farm in the whole county in all England—owned and operated by animals! Not one of them, not even the youngest, not even the newcomers who had been brought from farms ten or twenty miles away, ever ceased to marvel at that. And when they heard the gun booming and saw the green flag fluttering at the **masthead**③, their hearts swelled with **imperishable**④ pride, and the talk turned always towards the old heroic days, the expulsion of Jones, the writing of the Seven Commandments, the great battles in which the human invaders had been defeated. None of the old dreams had been abandoned. The Republic of the Animals which Major had foretold, when the green fields of England should be untrodden by human feet, was still believed in. Some day it was coming: it might not be soon, it might not be with in the lifetime of any animal now living, but still it was coming. Even the tune of *Beasts of England*

又非常之多，而且胃口一直都很好。

至于其他动物，他们心里清楚，自己的生活还是一如既往，大都处于饥饿状态，还是在干草上睡眠，在池塘里饮水，在田地里干活儿。冬天里，他们忍受严寒的痛苦。夏天里，他们饱受蚊虫的侵扰。有时候，他们当中年老的动物会绞尽脑汁，想要追忆一些昔日往事，设法想要弄清楚，反抗运动初期——当时琼斯刚刚被驱逐出农场——同现在相比，情况更好还是更坏。他们无法回忆起来。他们无法拿出什么东西同现在的生活相比。尖嗓子提供的数据总能够说明一切都在变得越来越好。除了尖嗓子那一串串数据之外，他们没有任何依据。动物们发现，这是个无法说清楚的问题。无论如何，他们现在也没有闲暇来考虑这些事情。只有年迈的本杰明声称自己记得漫长一生中的所有细节，而且知道，今昔相比，情况好不到哪儿，也坏不到哪儿——正如他说的，饥饿、艰辛、失望是生活中永不改变的规律。

尽管如此，动物们却从未放弃过希望。尤其是，他们须臾都没有丧失过自己作为动物农场成员所带来的荣誉感和优越感。他们所在的农场仍然是全郡全英国唯一一座——由动物们所有并管理着的农场。所有动物当中——哪怕是最年幼的，哪怕是那些从十英里或者二十英里外的农场买来的新来者——没有一个对此不感到惊叹的。他们听到礼炮鸣响，看到绿色旗帜在旗杆上高高飘扬。这种时候，他们的心中会产生无法抑制的自豪感。大家的话题就总会转向昔日那英雄的时代，琼斯遭到驱逐，写在墙壁上的"七戒"条文，令人类入侵者屡遭惨败的一次次场面宏大的战斗。动物们从未放弃过昔日的梦想。他们仍然相信少校曾经预言过的动物共和国，到时候，人类不得涉足英格兰郁郁葱葱的田野。有朝一日，这个目标一定会实现，或许那一天不会很快到来，或许动物们的有生之年看不到那一天的到来，但一定会到来

① rack [ræk] v. 绞尽脑汁

② invariably [in'vɛəriəbli] ad. 总是

③ masthead ['mɑ:sthed] n. 桅顶
④ imperishable [im'periʃəbl] a. 永存的

was perhaps hummed secretly here and there: at any rate, it was a fact that every animal on the farm knew it, though no one would have dared to sing it aloud. It might be that their lives were hard and that not all of their hopes had been fulfilled; but they were conscious that they were not as other animals. If they went hungry, it was not from feeding **tyrannical**[①] human beings; if they worked hard, at least they worked for themselves. No creature among them went upon two legs. No creature called any other creature "Master." All animals were equal.

One day in early summer Squealer ordered the sheep to follow him, and led them out to a piece of waste ground at the other end of the farm, which had become overgrown with birch **saplings**[②]. The sheep spent the whole day there browsing at the leaves under Squealer's supervision. In the evening he returned to the farmhouse himself, but, as it was warm weather, told the sheep to stay where they were. It ended by their remaining there for a whole week, during which time the other animals saw nothing of them. Squealer was with them for the greater part of every day. He was, he said, teaching them to sing a new song, for which privacy was needed.

It was just after the sheep had returned, on a pleasant evening when the animals had finished work and were making their way back to the farm buildings, that the terrified **neighing**[③] of a horse sounded from the yard. Startled, the animals stopped in their tracks. It was Clover's voice. She neighed again, and all the animals broke into a gallop and rushed into the yard. Then they saw what Clover had seen.

It was a pig walking on his hind legs.

Yes, it was Squealer. A little awkwardly, as though not quite used to supporting his considerable **bulk**[④] in that position, but with perfect balance, he was strolling across the yard. And a moment later, out from the door of the farmhouse came a long file of pigs, all walking on their hind legs. Some did it better than others, one or two were even a **trifle**[⑤] unsteady and looked as though they would have liked the support of a stick, but every one of them made his way right round the yard successfully. And finally there was a tremendous baying

的。动物们甚至在四处悄悄地哼唱着《英格兰的牲畜》的曲调。不管怎么说，农场上的所有动物都熟悉这旋律，这是事实。不过，没有任何动物敢高声唱出来。动物们的生活可能很艰难，他们的希望可能并非全部都实现了。但是，他们心里很清楚，他们和别的动物不一样。如果说他们要忍饥挨饿，那并不是因为他们供养了残暴的人类。如果说他们要拼命干活，他们至少是在替自己干活。他们中间没有用两条腿走路的，没有任何动物称其他动物为"主人"。所有动物一律平等。

初夏的一天，尖嗓子吩咐绵羊们跟着他，然后领着他们到了农场另一端的一片荒地，那儿长满了桦树苗。在尖嗓子的监督下，绵羊们在那儿待了一整天，吃着树叶。黄昏时分，尖嗓子自个儿返回到了住宅，但是，由于天气暖和，他告诉绵羊们待在原地。结果，绵羊在那儿待了整整一个星期，期间，其他动物未见他们的踪影。尖嗓子每天大部分时间里都和他们待在一块儿。他说，他在教他们唱一首新歌，为此，他们需要不受打扰的环境。

绵羊们返回后不久，一个美妙的黄昏，动物们刚收工，正返回农场的窝棚区。这时候，院落里传来马匹恐惧的嘶鸣声。动物们惊愕不已，停住了脚步。那是苜蓿的声音。她再次嘶鸣起来。动物们急忙冲进院落，看到了苜蓿看到的情形。

那是一头猪在用两条后腿站立着行走。

是啊，那头猪是尖嗓子。动作显得有点笨拙，好像还不大习惯于用那样的姿势支撑自己相当笨重的躯体。不过，他还是把身体平衡得十分完美，正大步走过院落。片刻之后，住宅门口走出长长一大溜猪，全部用两条后腿走路。有些猪比另外一些走得更加稳健，有一两头走路时显得有点摇晃，看上去好像需要拐杖的支撑。不过，每头猪都成功地绕着院落走了一圈。最后，传来那群狗疯狂的吠叫，那只黑公鸡尖声的啼鸣。紧接着，拿破仑

① tyrannical [ti'rænikəl] *a.* 专横的

② sapling ['sæpliŋ] *n.* 树苗

③ neigh [nei] *v.*（马）嘶

④ bulk [bʌlk] *n.*（尤指肥硕的）身躯

⑤ a trifle 有点儿

of dogs and a shrill crowing from the black cockerel, and out came Napoleon himself, majestically upright, casting **haughty**① glances from side to side, and with his dogs gambolling round him.

He carried a whip in his trotter.

There was a deadly silence. Amazed, terrified, huddling together, the animals watched the long line of pigs march slowly round the yard. It was as though the world had turned upside-down. Then there came a moment when the first shock had worn off and when, in spite of everything—in spite of their terror of the dogs, and of the habit, developed through long years, of never complaining, never criticising, no matter what happened—they might have uttered some word of protest. But just at that moment, as though at a signal, all the sheep burst out into a tremendous bleating of—

"Four legs good, two legs better! Four legs good, two legs better! Four legs good, two legs better!"

It went on for five minutes without stopping. And by the time the sheep had quieted down, the chance to utter any protest had passed, for the pigs had marched back into the farmhouse.

Benjamin felt a nose **nuzzling**② at his shoulder. He looked round. It was Clover. Her old eyes looked dimmer than ever. Without saying anything, she **tugged**③ gently at his mane and led him round to the end of the big barn, where the Seven Commandments were written. For a minute or two they stood gazing at the tarred wall with its white lettering.

"My sight is failing," she said finally. "Even when I was young I could not have read what was written there. But it appears to me that that wall looks different. Are the Seven Commandments the same as they used to be, Benjamin?"

For once Benjamin **consented**④ to break his rule, and he read out to her what was written on the wall. There was nothing there now except a single Commandment. It ran:

① haughty ['hɔːti] *a.* 傲慢的

现身了，他挺直着身子，耀武扬威，神情傲慢地左右扫视了一番，那群狗蹦跳着簇拥在他周围。

拿破仑的蹄子夹着一根鞭子。

动物群顿时一片寂静。动物们惊愕不已，诚惶诚恐，挤在一块儿。他们注视着长长一大溜猪绕着院落缓步前行。世界仿佛颠倒了。随后，动物们从最初的惊愕中慢慢缓过来了。尽管有种种原因——尽管他们恐惧那群狗，尽管长期以来，他们养成了习惯，不管发生了什么事情，从不抱怨，从不批评——但是，他们还是会发出抗议的声音。不过，就在这个当儿，好像是接收到了什么信号似的，所有绵羊突然大声咩咩地说出——

"四条腿好，两条腿更好！四条腿好，两条腿更好！四条腿好，两条腿更好！"

声音持续了五分钟，没有停顿过。等到绵羊平静下来了之后，表示抗议的机会已经失去了，因为那些猪已经进入到了室内。

② nuzzle ['nʌzl] *v.* （用鼻子）擦

本杰明感觉到有哪个动物用鼻子触碰了自己的肩膀，便扭过头看了看，原来是苜蓿。她的视力比先前越发模糊了。她没有开口说什么，只是轻柔地拽住他的鬃毛，领着他绕到大谷仓的一侧去，到了写"七戒"的那堵墙边。有一两分钟的时间，他们伫立在墙边，注视着柏油上面写着的白颜色的文字。

③ tug [tʌg] *v.* 拖曳

"我的视力越来越差了，"她最后说，"即便年轻时，我也认不清这面墙上写了些什么。但是，我寻思着，这墙上的字好像不一样了。这儿的'七戒'还跟过去的一样吗，本杰明？"

④ consent [kən'sent] *v.* 同意

本杰明唯有这次愿意打破自己定下的规矩，给苜蓿念出了墙上写着的文字。墙壁上除了"一戒"之外，其余的都没有了。"一戒"的内容是：

All animals are equal

But some animals are more equal than others

After that it did not seem strange when next day the pigs who were supervising the work of the farm all carried whips in their trotters. It did not seem strange to learn that the pigs had bought themselves a wireless set, were arranging to install a telephone, and had taken out **subscriptions**① to *John Bull, TitBits*, and the *Daily Mirror*. It did not seem strange when Napoleon was seen strolling in the farmhouse garden with a **pipe**② in his mouth, no, not even when the pigs took Mr. Jones's clothes out of the wardrobes and put them on, Napoleon himself appearing in a black coat, **ratcatcher**③ **breeches**④, and leather leggings, while his favourite sow appeared in the watered silk dress which Mrs. Jones had been used to wear on Sundays.

A week later, in the afternoon, a number of dogcarts drove up to the farm. A **deputation**⑤ of neighbouring farmers had been invited to make a tour of inspection. They were shown all over the farm, and expressed great admiration for everything they saw, especially the windmill. The animals were weeding the turnip field. They worked diligently hardly raising their faces from the ground, and not knowing whether to be more frightened of the pigs or of the human visitors.

That evening loud laughter and bursts of singing came from the farmhouse. And suddenly, at the sound of the mingled voices, the animals were stricken with curiosity. What could be happening in there, now that for the first time animals and human beings were meeting on terms of equality? With one accord they began to **creep**⑥ as quietly as possible into the farmhouse garden.

At the gate they paused, half frightened to go on but Clover led the way in. They tiptoed up to the house, and such animals as were tall enough peered in at the dining-room window. There, round the long table, sat half a dozen farmers and half a dozen of the more **eminent**⑦ pigs, Napoleon himself occupying the seat of honour at the head of the table. The pigs appeared completely at ease in

所有动物一律平等，

但有些动物比其他的更加平等。

这样一来，翌日，那些负责农场监工的猪全都在蹄子上夹着鞭子。此事似乎并不奇怪。动物们听说猪已经替自己购买了无线电收音机，准备安装电话，已经订阅了《约翰牛报》《趣闻荟萃》《每日镜报》。此事似乎并不奇怪。动物们看见拿破仑嘴上叼着烟斗在住宅的院落里散步，那些猪甚至把琼斯先生的衣服从衣柜里面拿出来，穿在自己身上。拿破仑出现时上身穿着黑色外套，下身穿着猎装裤，打着绑腿，而他最宠爱的那头母猪则穿着当初琼斯太太在星期天才穿的波纹丝绸衣服。此事也似乎并不奇怪。

一个星期过后，一天下午，许多轻便马车驶入了农场。附近的一些农场主组成的代表团应邀前来农场参观考察。主人们领着客人走遍了整个农场，客人们对所看到的情景大加赞赏，尤其对风车。动物们正在给萝卜地除草。他们辛勤地埋头干活儿，几乎连头都没有抬起来，不知道是更加惧怕那些猪呢，还是更加惧怕前来参观的人。

当晚，住宅里传出响亮的笑声和阵阵歌声。突然间，面对各种混杂的声音，动物们充满了好奇。那儿发生了什么情况，动物和人类竟然头一回平等相聚？他们想到一块儿了，开始尽可能悄然无声地进入住宅花园。

到达门口时，他们停住了脚步，有点不大敢继续向前走，但还是首蓿领头走了进去。他们踮着脚进入室内，个头高的动物对着餐厅窗户朝里面看。里面一张长条餐桌周围坐着五六个农场主和五六头有头有脸的猪。拿破仑自己坐在首席，显得很尊贵。猪坐在椅子上一副完全放松的样子。人畜聚集在一块儿，正兴致勃勃地玩着牌

① subscription [səb'skripʃən] n. 订阅

② pipe [paip] n. 烟斗

③ ratcatcher ['ræt.kætʃə] n. 狩猎装
④ breech [bri:tʃ] n. 下部

⑤ deputation [.depju'teiʃən] n. 代表团

⑥ creep [kri:p] v. 慢慢地移动

⑦ eminent ['eminənt] a. 显赫的

their chairs. The company had been enjoying a game of cards but had broken off for the moment, evidently in order to drink a toast. A large **jug**① was circulating, and the **mugs**② were being refilled with beer. No one noticed the wondering faces of the animals that gazed in at the window.

Mr. Pilkington, of Foxwood, had stood up, his mug in his hand. In a moment, he said, he would ask the present company to drink a toast. But before doing so, there were a few words that he felt it **incumbent**③ upon him to say.

It was a source of great satisfaction to him, he said—and, he was sure, to all others present—to feel that a long period of mistrust and misunderstanding had now come to an end. There had been a time, not that he, or any of the present company, had shared such sentiments, but there had been a time when the respected **proprietors**④ of Animal Farm had been regarded, he would not say with hostility, but perhaps with a certain measure of misgiving, by their human neighbours. Unfortunate incidents had occurred, mistaken ideas had been current. It had been felt that the existence of a farm owned and operated by pigs was somehow abnormal and was liable to have an unsettling effect in the neighbourhood. Too many farmers had assumed, without due enquiry, that on such a farm a spirit of **licence**⑤ and indiscipline would prevail. They had been nervous about the effects upon their own animals, or even upon their human employees. But all such doubts were now dispelled. Today he and his friends had visited Animal Farm and inspected every inch of it with their own eyes, and what did they find? Not only the most up-to-date methods, but a discipline and an orderliness which should be an example to all farmers everywhere. He believed that he was right in saying that the lower animals on Animal Farm did more work and received less food than any animals in the county. Indeed, he and his fellow-visitors today had observed many features which they intended to introduce on their own farms immediately.

He would end his remarks, he said, by emphasising once again the friendly feelings that **subsisted**⑥, and ought to subsist, between Animal Farm and its neighbours. Between pigs and human beings there was not, and there need not

① jug [dʒʌg] *n.* 大壶

② mug [mʌg] *n.* 大杯

③ incumbent [in'kʌmbənt] *a.*
有义务的

④ proprietor [prə'praiətə] *n.*
所有人

⑤ licence ['laisəns] *n.* 放纵

⑥ subsist [səb'sist] *v.* 存在

呢。但暂停了片刻，显然是为了相互祝酒。席间在传递着一个大酒壶，一个个大酒杯再次斟满了啤酒。动物们一张张充满了惊奇的脸在窗户边注视着，里面谁也没有注意到。

狐狸林农场的皮尔金顿先生站起身，手上端着大酒杯。他说，他等一会要给在场的各位敬酒。但是，在此之前，他觉得有几句话必须得说。

他说，他感到无比高兴，而且，他肯定，在场的各位也是如此——长期以来的不信任感和误解现在终于结束了。曾经有一段时期，他本人也好，在场的各位也罢，都不是有意要猜疑和误解，但确实曾经有过一段时间，动物农场备受尊敬的主人们受到过他们的人类邻居——他不说敌视，但或许可以说是某种程度的猜疑。一些很不幸的事情发生了，一些错误的观念盛行。大家都觉得，一座农场由猪拥有并且管理，这多少有点不大正常，而且会给周边地区带来不安定的影响。许许多多农场主未经调查便认为，这样的农场一定充斥着恣意妄为和秩序混乱的局面。他们忧心忡忡，担心影响他们自己的动物，甚至影响他们的人类雇员。但是，现在，所有这一切怀疑都烟消云散了。今天，他和他的朋友们参观了动物农场，亲眼看到了其中的每一寸土地，他们发现了什么呢？农场上不仅管理方式一流，而且纪律严明，秩序井然，堪称各地农场的楷模。他相信，比起本郡的任何动物，动物农场的下等动物干的活儿更多，得到的饲料更少。这样说是恰如其分的。事实上，他和今天同行的客人们注意到了许多特色，他们打算立刻引入到他们自己的农场上去。

他说，自己结束这一番讲话之前，拟再次强调动物农场和其邻居之间业已存在并应该继续存在下去的友好关系。猪和人类之间并不存在也没有必要存在任何利益

be, any clash of interests whatever. Their struggles and their difficulties were one. Was not the labour problem the same everywhere? Here it became apparent that Mr. Pilkington was about to spring some carefully prepared **witticism**① on the company, but for a moment he was too overcome by amusement to be able to utter it. After much choking, during which his various chins turned purple, he managed to get it out: "If you have your lower animals to **contend with**②," he said, "we have our lower classes!" This **bon mot**③ set the table in a roar; and Mr. Pilkington once again congratulated the pigs on the low rations, the long working hours, and the general absence of **pampering**④ which he had observed on Animal Farm.

And now, he said finally, he would ask the company to rise to their feet and make certain that their glasses were full. "Gentlemen," concluded Mr. Pilkington, "gentlemen, I give you a toast: To the prosperity of Animal Farm!"

There was enthusiastic cheering and stamping of feet. Napoleon was so **gratified**⑤ that he left his place and came round the table to **clink**⑥ his mug against Mr. Pilkington's before emptying it. When the cheering had died down, Napoleon, who had remained on his feet, intimated that he too had a few words to say.

Like all of Napoleon's speeches, it was short and to the point. He too, he said, was happy that the period of misunderstanding was at an end. For a long time there had been rumours circulated, he had reason to think, by some **malignant**⑦ enemy—that there was something **subversive**⑧ and even revolutionary in the outlook of himself and his colleagues. They had been credited with attempting to stir up rebellion among the animals on neighbouring farms. Nothing could be further from the truth! Their sole wish, now and in the past, was to live at peace and in normal business relations with their neighbours. This farm which he had the honour to control, he added, was a co-operative enterprise. The title-deeds, which were in his own possession, were owned by the pigs jointly.

He did not believe, he said, that any of the old suspicions still lingered, but certain changes had been made recently in the routine of the farm which should have the effect of promoting confidence stiff further. Hitherto the animals on the

① witticism ['witisizəm]

② contend with 对付

③ bon mot 妙语；警句

④ pampering ['pæmpəriŋ] *n.* 纵容

⑤ gratified ['grætifaid] *a.* 称心的

⑥ clink [kliŋk] *v.* 发出叮当声

⑦ malignant [mə'lignənt] *a.* 恶意的

⑧ subversive [səb'vɜːsiv] *a.* 破坏（性）的

冲突。他们要进行的斗争和要克服的困难是一致的。劳工问题不是每个地方都一样吗？至此，很显然，皮尔金顿先生拟在大家面前抛出精心准备好的一句调侃说辞，但一时间自己觉得忍俊不禁，话未能够说出口。呛了好一会儿，期间他的多层下颚胀得发紫，这才设法把话说出来了。"你们若是要对付下等动物，"他说，"我们也有下层阶级要对付呢！"这句形象隽永的话令餐桌边的主客哄堂大笑起来。皮尔金顿先生已经观察到，动物农场饲料配额低，干活儿时间长，但却毫无松懈拖沓现象。他再次向那些猪表示祝贺。

至此，他最后说，请求大家站起身，确认酒杯是满的。"先生们，"皮尔金顿先生说，"先生们，我敬你们大家一杯：祝愿动物农场繁荣昌盛！"

现场顿时响起热情洋溢的欢呼声和跺脚声。拿破仑感激不已，他离开自己的座位绕过餐桌，同皮尔金顿先生碰了杯，随即饮下了杯中酒。欢呼声平息之后，拿破仑仍然站立着，表示他也有几句话要说。

如同拿破仑平常的说话风格一样，他这次说的话也很简明扼要。他说，他也高兴地看到，误解的时代过去了。长期以来，总是谣言四起——他有理由觉得，这是某些险恶的敌人所为——说他本人和他的同事们观念当中有颠覆甚至革命的思想。说他们图谋在附近农场的动物中煽动反抗运动。这不是事实，纯属子虚乌有！无论是现在还是过去，他们唯一的愿望是，与邻居和平共处，展开正常的业务关系。他补充说，自己很荣幸管理着的这座农场是一个团结协作的企业。由他本人保管的那些地契归猪共同所有。

他说，他相信，尽管任何昔日的猜疑都不可能继续存在下去，但是，农场最近还是对处理事务的惯例做了一些更改，旨在进一步增强信任。迄今为止，农场上的

farm had had a rather foolish custom of addressing one another as "Comrade." This was to be **suppressed**①. There had also been a very strange custom, whose origin was unknown, of marching every Sunday morning past a boar's skull which was nailed to a post in the garden. This, too, would be suppressed, and the skull had already been buried. His visitors might have observed, too, the green flag which flew from the masthead. If so, they would perhaps have noted that the white hoof and horn with which it had previously been marked had now been removed. It would be a plain green flag from now onwards.

He had only one criticism, he said, to make of Mr. Pilkington's excellent and neighbourly speech. Mr. Pilkington had referred throughout to "Animal Farm". He could not of course know, for he, Napoleon, was only now for the first time announcing it, that the name "Animal Farm" had been abolished. Henceforward the farm was to be known as "The Manor Farm"—which, he believed, was its correct and original name.

"Gentlemen," concluded Napoleon, "I will give you the same toast as before, but in a different form. Fill your glasses to the brim. Gentlemen, here is my toast: To the prosperity of The Manor Farm!"

There was the same hearty cheering as before, and the mugs were emptied to the **dregs**②. But as the animals outside gazed at the scene, it seemed to them that some strange thing was happening. What was it that had altered in the faces of the pigs? Clover's old dim eyes **flitted**③ from one face to another. Some of them had five chins, some had four, some had three. But what was it that seemed to be melting and changing? Then, the applause having come to an end, the company took up their cards and continued the game that had been interrupted, and the animals crept silently away.

But they had not gone twenty yards when they stopped short. An uproar of voices was coming from the farmhouse. They rushed back and looked through the window again. Yes, a violent quarrel was in progress. There were shoutings, **bangings**④ on the table, sharp suspicious glances, furious denials. The source of the trouble appeared to be that Napoleon and Mr. Pilkington had each played an

① suppress [sə'pres] *v.* 禁止

动物之间互称"同志",这是个很愚蠢的惯例。这个惯例应该废止。还有一种很不可思议的惯例,如何形成的无从查考,即花园里树干上用钉子固定着一具公猪的骷髅,每个星期天的上午动物们要列队走过那儿。这个惯例也应该废止。那具骷髅已经掩埋掉了。他的客人们可能已经看到了飘扬在旗杆顶端的那面绿色旗帜。情况若是如此,他们或许可以注意到,先前绘制在上面的兽蹄和兽角已经没有了。从今往后,上面飘扬着的是一面一抹光的绿色旗帜。

他说,对于皮尔金顿先生精彩而又友好的讲话,他只有一处需要指出的。皮尔金顿先生的通篇讲话都提到了"动物农场"。他当然不知道,因为他,拿破仑,现在第一次公布,"动物农场"这个名字取消了。从今往后,农场名叫"庄园农场"——他相信,这才是其正确和原有的名字。

"先生们,"拿破仑最后说,"我要和前面一样,向你们敬酒,但用不同的说辞。斟满你们的酒杯吧。先生们,我的祝酒词是:祝愿庄园农场繁荣昌盛!"

② to the dregs 精光,一点不剩

和先前一样,现场一片热情洋溢的欢呼声,大家把杯中酒一饮而尽。但是,动物们在外面注视着现场情景的当儿,他们似乎觉得,里面正在发生着什么不可思议的事情。猪的脸上到底发生了什么变化呢?苜蓿老眼昏

③ flit [flit] *v.* 掠过

花,目光从一张脸掠到另一张。有的脸上长着五个下颚,有的四个,有的三个。但是,那似乎在融化和变化着的是什么东西呢?然后,掌声停止了,在场各位拿起自己的牌,继续从刚才中断的地方玩游戏。动物们悄无声息地离开了。

但是,动物们还没有走出二十码远,他们突然停住了。农场主住宅里传出喧闹的声音。动物们往回冲,再次在窗口张望。是啊,里面正激烈地争吵着呢。高声大气的喊声,对着餐桌砰砰的敲击声,犀利的怀疑目光,怒气冲冲的矢口否认。争吵的起因似乎是,拿破仑和皮

④ banging ['bæŋiŋ] *n.* 猛敲

ace of **spades**① simultaneously.

Twelve voices were shouting in anger, and they were all alike. No question, now, what had happened to the faces of the pigs. The creatures outside looked from pig to man, and from man to pig, and from pig to man again; but already it was impossible to say which was which.

THE END

① spade ['speid] *n.*（纸牌的中）黑桃

尔金顿先生同时出了一张黑桃 A。

十二个嗓门愤怒地吼着，声音全部变成一样的了。是啊，猪的脸到底是怎么回事，已经没有疑问了。外面的动物们把目光从猪移到人身上，从人移到猪身上，再从猪移到人身上。但是，谁是谁，已经不可能分辨得清楚了。